ARCHERY 4 KIDS

ARCHERY 4 KIDS

KIDS

by **Steve Ruis**
Editor of
Archery Focus Magazine

WATCHING ARROWS FLY, LLC

Library of Congress Cataloging-in Publication Data

Archery for Kids / Steve Ruis.
　　p. cm
　　Includes bibliographic references and index.
　　ISBN 978-0-9821471-7-7 (softcover)
　　1. Archery. 2. Youth. I Steve Ruis, 1946-

ISBN: 978-0-9821471-7-7

The web addresses cited in this text were current as of August 2010, unless otherwise noted.

Writer: Steve Ruis; **Copy Editor**: Steve Ruis; **Proofreader**: Claudia Stevenson; **Graphic Artist**: Steve Ruis; **Cover Designer**: Steve Ruis; **Photographers** (cover and interior): Steve Ruis and Claudia Stevenson unless otherwise noted; **Illustrator** Steve Ruis

Printed in the United States of America 10 9 8 7 6 5 4 3 2 1

Watching Arrows Fly
3712 North Broadway, #285
Chicago, IL 60613
800.671.1140

Dedication

This book is dedicated to Jim Easton, a man who has tirelessly dedicated his life and his passion to the sport of archery. This is especially true of his desire to see young people have the opportunity to participate in the sport and experience the joy a bow and arrow can bring to young lives.

Steve Ruis
September 2010

Steve Ruis

Table of Contents

Preface

Since you are reading this, I assume that you have tried archery, are jazzed by it, and are curious to find out more! In this book I will introduce you to the world of target archery for beginners.

I will walk you through the basics of archery safety, bows and arrows (and other archery gear), how to shoot, competing, and how to go about getting your own gear and finding a coach or instructor!

Each chapter is short. (I know you would rather be shooting arrows than reading about shooting them.) And each chapter is followed by the most common questions I get from beginners (with answers!).

I wrote this books for kids ages 8-14, but I guess it is okay for you adult beginners to read it, too. (Hey, I started archery when I was 43!)

If you are not a beginner and have been shooting awhile, you may be better off with another book. If you own your own equipment, you might be interested in **Precision Archery** (Human Kinetics, 2003) that my partner Claudia Stevenson and I created for intermediate archers (and up).

If instead of *being* a kid, you *work with* kids teaching them archery, you may be more interested in **Coaching Archery** (Watching Arrows Fly, 2009). I wrote Coaching Archery for all of you beginning-to-intermediate archery

1

coach/instructors.

If you are a hot shot archer and you want to learn how to win, I will soon be publishing a book called **Winning Archery**, providing aspiring archers with all of the information necessary to learn how to win consistently which has been left out of all of the other books!

And if you *have* kids who are getting interested in archery, look for **A Parent's Guide to Archery** which is being published right now.

Let's get started!

Steve Ruis
Chicago, Illinois
September 2010

Preface Q & A s

Q I love archery! Can I shoot in my neighborhood park?

A If your park has an archery program, yes! If you are asking because you want to just go out and shoot, the answer is "no." In many communities doing this is illegal. In most communities this is unsafe. In general, you should only be shooting arrows at an authorized archery range (permanent or temporary) set up by a certified coach/instructor. There are private (club) ranges all over the country and ranges in archery shops. Check with the Parks and Recreation people in your area to see if they offer archery. Many summer camps offer archery, too.

Q How hard is it to become a really good archer?

A It depends. Some kids can win competitions within just a few months of starting the sport. The key is to practice a lot under the direction of a good coach.

I have a friend who got into archery because her two sons loved it. She started with a compound bow and after about a year and a half, she was told by a fellow archer that if she switched to shooting a recurve bow, and worked with a coach, she could do very well in competitions. She practiced a great deal and six months later she was representing the United States in Croatia as a member of our World Field Archery Team! Three years later, she became the Women's World Field Champion. She was 51 years old.

Young or old, great progress can be made with dedicated practice.

Q Where . . . ?

A Hold on, hold on. All will be made clear in the coming
chapters. Start reading!

Archery 4 Kids

Chapter 1
Safety!

Oh no, you thought we were going to start with bows and arrows, didn't you? Well, we can't and that's because learning to shoot arrows from bows is a form of weapons training. It is important that you and those around you know the safe use of bows and arrows. You or other people around you could get hurt otherwise. So, please do not skip over this chapter! This is the most important chapter in the book.

Despite the appearance of being dangerous, archery is one of the *safest* sports around. Do you know why?

Archery is safe because *everyone learns safe habits*. When everyone has safe habits, safety is a sure thing and no one has to even think about it. Safety just happens, because "that's the way we do things."

Yes, there are some rules to learn, but they are few and kind of obvious, so don't worry. What you need to know first is the primary safety rule of archery—*you are only allowed to do the things we say you can*. Now, your parents tell you there are things you can do and things you can't do. And if something you want to do isn't a definite "can" or "can't" you have to decide which it is. In archery, the only things you can do are the things allowed. Period.

There are no decisions to make. There are no "can'ts" only "cans."

The reason for this is there are way too many "can'ts." The list of "no can do's" is really, really long. And before you learned them all, you could get into trouble. For example, you can't shoot arrows at people. Or at pets. Or at wild animals. Or at ponds. Or at rocks. Or at trees. Or at a house. Or at a garage. The list of things you can't shoot an arrow at is endless.

We solve this with one simple rule: *you may only shoot at indicated targets.* Ta da! Don't even ask about shooting at anything else. All of the other safety rules are similar. We say what you *can* do, and that is *all* you can do.

Also, we will train you to do certain things in certain ways. We will teach you a safe way to do everything and then, as you repeat that thing, you are building a safe habit.

So, here are the rules!

The Basic Safety Rules

- Know and obey all range commands.
- Keep your arrows in your quiver until you are told you can shoot.
- Always wear an armguard.
- Only use the arrows you have been given to use.
- Always point your arrows at a target.
- Only draw a bow with an arrow in it.
- Only shoot at indicated targets.
- If you drop an arrow, you may pick it up only if you can do so without moving your feet; otherwise leave it where it fell.
- Always walk at the archery range.
- Obey all whistle system commands.
- Only pull arrows by approved procedures.

Because these are so important I am going to explain each of them in detail.

Know and obey all range commands. This one is obvious but you need to know that archery ranges often post their own "Range Rules." Be sure to read these as there may be some new rules to obey. Archery coaches and instructors can add to the rules above or to the rules posted. We teach our instructors to always post their extra rules so they are easier to learn, but not everyone does this. So, you need to obey all of the posted and oral commands.

Keep your arrows in your quiver until you are told you can shoot. You may wear a quiver, usually hung at your side. Or you may have a "ground quiver" to use. A ground quiver may be anything from a piece of plastic pipe, to an orange safety cone, or even just a spot on the ground. This is where your arrows are kept when you are not shooting them.

Always wear an armguard. An armguard protects

Quivers come in all sizes and shapes and can be worn or just stand by you on the shooting line. Some traditional archers even use the same quiver Robin Hood did.

your forearm from an accidental slap from the bowstring. Getting hit by a bowstring is like being whipped—it really hurts! All beginners must wear armguards to protect against this problem. You may also want to use a "finger tab." Finger tabs protect your fingers from the pressure of the bowstring. Many beginners prefer not to use a tab until their fingers get sore. We only require tabs for students whose fingers begin to get sore. Your program may require a tab all of the time.

Only use the arrows you have been given to use. If someone offers an arrow for you to shoot, just say "no." Arrows that are the wrong size can be very dangerous! When you are provided archery program arrows or sold arrows to use, the arrows are sized to be safe. A borrowed arrow hasn't been likewise chosen and may be dangerous to shoot.

armguard (large is good)

chest protector (string guard)

finger tab

Always point your arrows at a target. The only place you can load an arrow on your bow is when you are on the shooting line. You won't be given permission to shoot an arrow until you are standing on the line correctly. If you point the arrow somewhere other than at your target, accidents can happen. So, we teach the habit of always pointing the arrow at the only thing you are allowed to shoot. This actually becomes a habit of shooting form. It becomes a habit so quickly, you may have trouble recalling the rule! You will just always do it that way.

Only draw a bow with an arrow on it. This means when you are on the shooting line and it is safe. The only exception to this rule is if your instructor or coach asks

11

you to pull a bow to see if it suits you. What they are look-ing for is whether you can pull the bow using good archery form without grimacing, grunting, or sweating, so use your best form and draw the bow as instructed. Be sure to hang onto the bowstring! If you let the string go when there is no arrow attached (this is called a "dry fire") you can break the bow and/or hurt yourself! This is why the rule "Only draw the bow with an arrow on it." exists.

Only shoot at indicated targets. This one was dis-cussed at length at the beginning of this chapter. In short, there are way too many things you "can't" shoot, so we just say what you can.

If you drop an arrow, you may pick it up only if you can do so without moving your feet; *otherwise leave it where it fell.* This is a long one, but it is simple. If you get in the habit of stepping in front of the shooting line when you drop an arrow, you are in danger! Even just *one* step is bad. Because if you get used to taking *one* step to pick up a dropped arrow, you might take *two.* If *two* steps are okay, you will end up *three* or *four* steps in front of the line without thinking and you could get shot by another archer. This rule is simple and will always keep you safe. A dropped arrow can always be picked up when the com-mand to retrieve your arrows is given.

Always walk at the archery range. You will walk. You may not skip, jump, run, jog, ramble, saunter, or boogie on an archery range. If you run to a target to see your score and you trip, you may be pierced by the arrows sticking out of the target. If you trip and fall, you can get hurt by the arrows in your hip quiver. Since the ground on archery ranges is often rough, we walk carefully to avoid such accidents.

Obey all whistle system commands. Ordinary commands are typically given to a group of archers by whistle. These same commands are used around the world. If you have seen archery at the Olympics on TV or your computer, the "whistle" commands are made with an air horn so that everyone on the big field can hear them. Here are the "whistle commands."

The Whistle System

Two Blasts Archers may come to the shooting line.

One Blast Archers may place an arrow on their bows and begin shooting.

Three Blasts Archers may walk to the target to retrieve their arrows.

Five or More Blasts Emergency let down! Stop immediately and wait for instructions.

If you get an Emergency Let Down Command, you must not shoot! A "let down" is performed by pointing the arrow at the ground (outdoors) or the target immediately in front of you (indoors) and easing the string back to its undrawn position. Put the arrow back into its quiver and wait for instructions.

Only pull arrows by approved procedures. You have walked to the target to see your shot arrows. You have noted their scores. Now what? Now you will be directed to "pull your arrows." The pulling of arrows is actually where most of the accidents occur, so there is a standard procedure. When it is your turn:

1. Stand on the side of the target that allows you to pull with your "strong arm." (If you are right-handed, stand on the left side of the target. You will pull with your right arm. If you are a "leftie," it is the other way around.)

2. Check the "Danger Zone" (the space right in front of the target) to make sure you won't poke anyone when you pull your arrows.
3. Put your strong hand on top of the arrow you want to pull and slide it all the way to the target.
4. Put your other hand flat against the target where the arrow is sticking.
5. Grasp the arrow with your strong hand and pull straight back.

Always look over your shoulder to make sure you won't poke anybody when you pull (upper left). Off hand against target, grabbing arrow from on top, pull (upper right)! If you have a quiver, put each arrow away before you pull another; if not drop them on the ground as you pull them (lower left). Ask for help if you are struggling to pull your arrows; arrows above the level of your shoulders are expecially hard to pull (lower right)!

14

This should be demonstrated for you by your archery instructor/coach (*also see the photos left*). Pulling arrows should always be supervised by your instructor, so if you have a problem, ask for help. (Asking for help pulling an arrow is common. I still do it! Some times when arrows are really stuck it takes two people to pull them out!)

Once you have pulled an arrow, if you are wearing a hip quiver, put it in the quiver. If you are not carrying a quiver, drop the pulled arrow on the ground in front of the target. (Pulling another arrow with an arrow in your hand can damage both arrows! If you don't notice the damage and shoot them again . . . yes, it is dangerous.) Once you have pulled all of your arrows, pick them all up and line up their points in a bundle (*see photo below*). You can then carry them back to the shooting line but you must *always, always carry them in only one hand*! Your one hand must be wrapped around the points! If you do this and you trip, or someone stumbles into you, you cannot be hurt by the arrows if you hang on to them. It is physically impossible to poke yourself in the eye. It is pretty much impossible to poke yourself anywhere else if you just hang on. If you carry them with two hands, you could accidently let go of the points and . . . yes, it is dangerous! The habit you want to create is that you do not take the first step back to the target until your "bouquet of arrows" is made

and in just one hand or all of your arrows are in your quiver. (If you start walking before you are set, you can trip before the arrows are safe.)

Create these habits and you will always be safe.

Getting hurt is no fun, no fun at all.

Everyone at the target is in charge of safety. Even if it isn't your turn to pull, you need to keep yourself and others out of the "Danger Zone."

There are more rules, lots more, but almost all of these are rules of fair competition, rules to do archery competitions by. And, if you watch adult archers, you will see that some of these safety rules seem to be being broken. For example, one archer may offer another archer an arrow to shoot. This is considered safe for experts to do because they know how to size arrows and they won't accept an arrow that seems dangerous to shoot.

Another example is that expert archers occasionally pull arrows with an arrow in their pulling hand. (They have learned how to do it without the arrows touching each other.)

Because of this, *just because someone else is doing something doesn't make it safe for you to do so*! If you create the habits we are teaching, you will be safe . . . always. And you won't even have to think about it!

To be in one of my archery programs, you have to agree to live by these rules. You, not your parent or guardian, have to agree. I will hold you accountable and will toss you out of the program if you violate the rules you agreed to obey. Okay, I am not an ogre. Kids do get second chances . . . but never a third chance. I don't want to have nightmares about accidents I could have prevented by teaching you safe habits, and requiring you to learn them.

What About Pulling Arrows on a Field Range?

A field range requires you to carry your bow with you from where you shot your arrows to where you are going to pull them (the target). You need two hands to pull your arrows, so. . . .

Many field ranges provide "bow racks" at each target for you to hang your bow on for just this reason (*see photo*). If no bow rack is provided, you must lean your bow against the target butt, or use a stand you brought along, either works well.

If you get lazy and try to pull your arrows one-handed, while carrying your bow, all kinds of bad things can happen. Rack your bow or prop it and use both hands to pull.

Photo Courtesy of Andy Macdonald

Pulling two arrows at once (as this archer is doing) is a recipe for disaster—both arrows can be damaged. Trust me, this guy does not want to damage his arrows, especially since they cost about $30 a piece! This is an expert archer who has learned how to do this, but just because you see someone else do this, doesn't mean you can! Pull your arrows one at a time and you will have no problems. Many archery champions do this . . . as a matter of habit.

Chapter 1 Q & A s

Q I love archery! Can I shoot in my back yard?

A Generally the answer is "no." In many communities this is illegal. In most communities this is unsafe. Imagine how your neighbor would feel if he found one of your arrows in his back yard! Now, if you live on a farm and your parents can set up a place to shoot that is away from people and animals, the answer might be different (but might be the same).

In general, you should only be shooting arrows at an authorized archery range (permanent or temporary).

Q Can I let my little brother try archery?

A It depends. In general kids don't start archery until they are eight years old. Kids under eight sometimes don't have the physical strength to pull a bow. Other times young kids can't be trusted to obey the safety rules.

You can get him a tryout, though. If you are taking an archery class, ask your instructor if he/she will check out whether your little brother is ready for archery. If your instructor can't do this, another place to get him a try is at a "fun shoot." Fun shoots are put on at county fairs, archery ranges, city parks, and county recreation areas. We often let "little ones" try a shot at our fun shoots (see the photos below). Some can do it, some cannot.

You should not, repeat *not*, try to teach your little brother, friends, enemies, elves or orcs . . . really, anyone else to shoot. The starting age for being an archery instructor is 15, and then there is a training program you need to take. That program teaches you how to teach others . . . safely.

Which, if any, of these little archers are "too little"? Two of them shot bull's-eyes. Any? Actually **all** *of them are too little. The ones successful in hitting the target had help pulling the bow from their instructor. It is at "fun shoots" like this that they can try archery and see if they are up to the task.*

Q My Mom and Dad won't let me take my bow and arrows on the bus. I can only shoot when they drive me to the archery range. Please explain to them this is safe because I always obey the safety rules.

A Congratulations on getting your own archery gear! And, I live in Chicago and everyone gets around by bus and train. But I don't let my young students carry archery equipment on the bus or train. You never know who you will meet on a bus, or at a bus stop, or on the way to a bus stop. We provide lockers for kids to store their gear while taking lessons indoors. You might ask if you can store your gear safely at your local range and then you can just take yourself on the bus with no danger to you or anyone else.

Steve Ruis

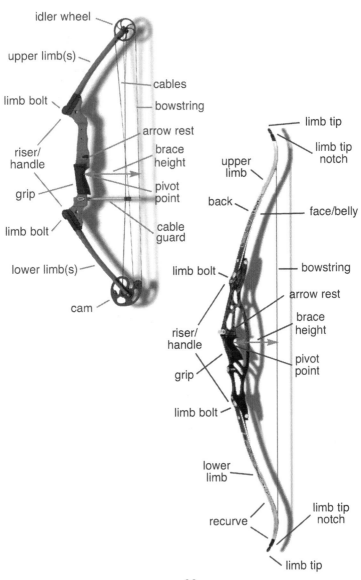

22

Chapter 2
Bows!

Nobody knows who the first person to make a bow was. Tying a string onto the two ends of a springy stick doesn't seem real obvious. Certainly this had to come after the invention of "string" and the invention of the spear. Yeah, the spear, because what is an arrow but a tiny spear launched faster than a big one? I imagine that at first there were long sticks (a staff) used as an aid for walking and as weapons (whack, whack). Then someone scraped a point on the stick with a sharp rock and made a thrusting spear (jab, jab). Then some prehistoric genius decided it worked by throwing it (a throwing spear). Then some

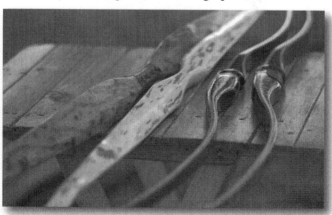

mega-genius got the idea of launching small spears (arrows) using a bent stick with a string attached (a bow)!

In any case, most believe the bow to have been invented well over 10,000 years ago! The really amazing thing is that the same basic bow design was being used by competitive archers up to about 1950! That design is called the "longbow." (I was so naïve when I first started archery to think "longbows" were so-named because they were, well, longer than "shortbows," whatever they were.) Bows dated to thousands of years ago show some quite sophisticated thinking going into their design. Even so, longbows have been improved little by little over the many, many years since their invention. And people today are still trying to improve their design!

The longbow was displaced by "recurve bows" in about 1950. The reasons were that recurve bows launched arrows faster and more consistently than longbows. You probably expected me to say they were "more accurate," but bows basically don't provide accuracy . . . archers do. Bows just launch arrows, archers point them.

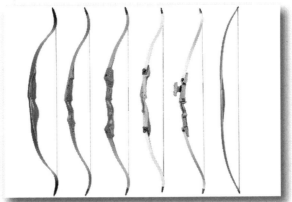

Recurve bows come as "one piece" (the two on the left) and "three piece" (the next three). Longbows may have a "shelf" like this bow (right) or not.

24

Modern day Olympic archers still use recurve bows. The design of these bows have been steadily modified since the invention of the recurve bow. The major improvements in the bows have been improvements in the materials used to make them more than in their design. Because of this, you will see that recurve bows from 1950 and today "look" very much the same. They are quite different, though, in what they are made of and how they perform.

Around about 1970, a gentleman named Hollis Allen (from Missouri) invented the first compound bow. It was immediately rejected by almost everyone because . . . it was ugly (*see photo below right*)! People then were shooting beautiful recurve bows made of exotic hardwoods (*see photo below left for an example*). The compound bow was an ugly contraption with pulleys and cables. (People actually debated whether it could even be called a bow!)

But the genius of the compound bow was that when you pulled the bow's string, the pulleys provided a mechanical advantage in pulling the bow. Part of the way back, it actually got *easier* to pull the string rather than harder! The vast majority of bows sold in the U.S. now are compound bows because of this wondrous design. They spit out arrows much faster with less effort than any comparable recurve or longbow.

If you want to see some cool old bows, check out *www.archeryhistory.com* for photos and descriptions.

In the rest of this chapter, I am going to discuss in more detail first recurve bows, then compound bows, then longbows. I will tell you why they are special. I will tell you why you might want to shoot such bows. And I will tell you what to look for when selecting such bows to shoot.

Let's explore bows!

Recurve Bows

Recurve bows basically come in two kinds: one-piece recurves and three-piece recurves. (Yes, there are two-piece recurves. But they are generally meant for back-packing bowhunters. And we don't have the space to cover every little bit of the "recurve bow picture.") We are going to concentrate on three-piece recurves because if you have a one-piece recurve and you want to shoot a longer low, you have to buy another bow. If you want to shoot a bow harder or easier to pull, you have to buy another bow. Three-piece recurve bows can be turned into longer or shorter or stronger or weaker bows by just replacing parts of the bow. So they are much cheaper and are more adjustable than one piece bows.

Three Piece Recurve Bows Three piece recurve bows consist of three pieces (duh!). The center part is called the "riser" or "handle." At both ends are the "limbs" (*see photo*).

Each "limb" is bolted or clipped onto the handle to make the bow. First, the limbs had actual bolts attaching them to the handle. Later these bolts (sensibly called "limb bolts") were redesigned so they could move the

26

limbs into slightly different positions. These different limb positions affect how hard the bowstring is to pull. Eventually, the limbs were redesigned so that they clipped onto the limb bolts. No more was it necessary to remove the bolts (turn, turn, turn, turn, . . .), attach the limbs, and then re-insert the bolts (turn, turn, turn, turn, . . .). Modern bows are therefore much easier to assemble: click, click, done!

You can leave the bow assembled, but for traveling back and forth to the archery range it is really convenient to be able to break the bow down into a smaller package.

Most of the least expensive bows still use the older "bolt-on" limb design (turn, turn, turn, turn, . . . turn, turn, turn) as these are easier and cheaper to make. This is actually good for beginners because it makes those bows cheaper to buy. But most archers eventually invest in the more easily assembled and more adjustable models (and more expensive) bows.

In addition to the limb bolts, the riser/handle generally comes with a place to attach an arrow rest. No, an arrow rest is not a place arrows take naps. Arrow rests are places for the arrow to "sit" while being shot. There are also screw holes in the riser to attach stabilizers, bow sights, and a "clicker" (*see Chapter 3*). These holes have been standardized, for the most part, but occasionally you can have a "Metric or English" thread problem.

The most important part of the bow is the "grip." The name is funny because you don't grip the bow! A handshake is a "grip" where you grasp and squeeze someone's hand. There is no "squeeze" when you hold a bow. Your "bow hand" cradles the bow at the grip position. But . . . the shape of the bow's grip affects how well you can do just that.

The three-piece recurve bow really shines when you decide you want to make changes. Let's say you grew a couple of inches in height and now you need a longer bow. The handle parts come in different lengths, typically 23″ and 25″ long. (Yes, there are other lengths. I am really tall, so I have a 27″ riser on my bow, for example. I have a 10-year old student with a 21″ riser. Also, even shorter bow handles are made for smaller kids, so you will have a lot of choices.) So, if you grew two inches and there is a handle that is two inches longer, you can buy just a new handle and Bingo! you now have a new, longer bow. This is much cheaper than buying a whole bow.

If you already have a long handle, the limbs come in three lengths: typically short, medium, and long. If you grew several inches and you had "short" limbs, you could replace them with "medium" limbs. Now you now have a bow that is two inches longer and you are good to go. (Generally you need one more inch of bow length for each two inches you grow taller.) Typically new limbs or a new handle costs about half of what a whole bow would cost.

And, if you develop your archery form and technique and grow your archery muscles, it may be to your advantage to shoot a bow requiring a stronger pull. (The pulling force of a bow is called its "draw weight" because we measure the pulling force in pounds.) If you want more drawing force in your bow, you can replace the limbs of the same length, with limbs rated as having more draw force needed to bend them. (Typically limbs are available in two pound (#) increments: like 24#, 26#, 28#, etc.) And Bingo! moving to higher draw weight limbs creates a stouter bow without the expense of buying a whole new bow.

You can see why three-piece bows are the most popular of the recurve bows and why beginners are recommended to consider them first.

We always start beginners on recurve bows because they are relatively light weight, easy to shoot, easy to learn on, and inexpensive. When you are selecting bows to shoot, here is what we recommend.

About as Tall as You Are If you stand a strung recurve bow on your shoe top, the other tip should come to a height somewhere between your chin and your eyes. (You never place the tip on the ground.) That is the recommend length. We will talk about buying your own archery gear in Chapter 5. In that chapter you will learn that, if you are still growing in height, you can go a little longer as you will need that length when you grow taller.

Start with the Lowest Draw Weight You Can Use When it comes to how much draw weight you want in a bow, less is more. When you are learning how to shoot, if the bow is too hard to pull, you won't be able to use good archery form to draw the bow. This will actually make you a worse archer! Don't fall into the trap of wanting to brag about pulling the stoutest bow in class. Besides, it will just be embarrassing when someone pulling less weight out-shoots you!

Here is a test to tell if the bow you are using has too little, too much, or just the right amount of draw weight. This test was developed by Coach Kim, H.T. of Korea (*see photos next page*):

The Draw Weight Test

Draw your bow to anchor, hold for seven seconds comfortably, then let down to predraw position (3-4 inches of draw) for two seconds. If you can do this eight times in succession without strain, your draw weight is correct. If you can only do this 3-4 times, it will be difficult to learn to shoot well. If you can do this ten times, your draw weight can be increased.

As a safety rule, you should only draw a bow while you have an arrow on the bow. For the purposes of this test, you may draw the bow without an arrow on it (always check with your archery instructor first) and be sure to hold on to the string! If you let the string go when there is no arrow attached (this is called a "dry fire") you can break the bow and/or hurt yourself.

Compound Bows

You may already have shot a compound bow if you have shot a *Genesis* bow. The Mathews *Genesis* bow is the most common bow used in beginning archery classes involving

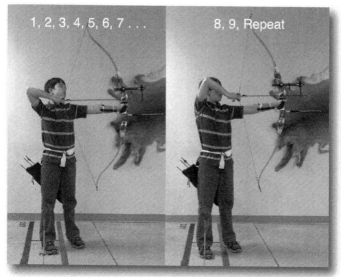

The Draw Weight Test—*10+ times in a row: more draw weight is acceptable, 8 times: just right, only 3-4 maybe too much draw weight. Try this with borrowed bows and figure out your own "best draw weight." This will change over time (with practice) so do the test as often as you need to to see if your draw weight still is best for you.*

compound bows. It is used exclusively in National Archery in the Schools Program (NASP) schools. Actually the *Genesis* compound bow is not a "true" compound bow. (I can only explain this by explaining how compound bows work.)

How Compound Bows Work All compound bows work the same way. But there are a great many different designs making use of this idea.

Here is the basic situation using what is called a "two cam" bow as an example. At the tips of the compound bow's limbs are mounted pulleys (also called "cams"). The bowstring is attached to both cams but to nothing else. Each cam has another string attached to it, called a

31

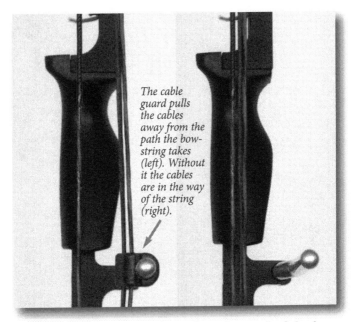

The cable guard pulls the cables away from the path the bowstring takes (left). Without it the cables are in the way of the string (right).

"cable." Each cable extends to the other end of the bow where it attaches to the limb tip. So the cam at the top limb's tip is attached to the bowstring and to a cable that runs down and is attached to the bottom limb. The cam at the bottom limb's tip is attached to the bowstring and to a cable that runs up and is attached to the bottom limb. The cables are very close (too close) to the bowstring. They would interfere with the arrow if left where they are so they are generally pulled off to the side (*see photos*). Typically the cables are pulled off to one side of a stiff rod (called a "cable guide" or "cable guard") inserted into the riser/handle. This is often done with a plastic slide (called a "cable slide") or, the most modern way, allowed to run around small pulleys on the tip of a cable guard.

When the bowstring is pulled, the cams must rotate

on their axles. The axles are placed off center so that when the cams rotate, the cables are pulled up above the limb tip and this bends the bow's limbs. The magic happens when you get close to "full draw" position. At some point the cable attachment point has gotten as far from the axle as it can get. It then rotates a bit farther and . . . the draw force, the amount of "pull" you need, actually goes down!

Each limb is holding part of the draw force for you at full draw. The only force you have to apply is just enough to turn the cams. The cams bend the limbs with the mechanical advantage designed into them. This lessening of the draw force needed is called "let-off." Typically, less than half of the force needed to reach the maximum amount remains at full draw. See the photo strips below showing the draw force as the bow is drawn. A handheld digital draw force gauge reads out the force in pounds.

At brace there is zero force and then it climbs up rapidly to the peak weight (42#) but then "lets off" to just 14# at full draw.

In the second photo series you can see the same thing

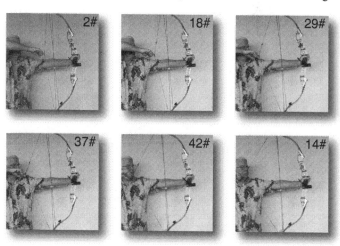

done with a *Genesis* bow. The *Genesis* design is a "one cam" design. All of the limb bending is done by the cam at the bottom. (This is why it has such an elaborate shape.) The bowstring is really long and it attaches to the cam at the bottom. It then runs up to the top where it goes over a round wheel and back to the bottom. It re-attaches to the cam in a different place. There is just one short cable. This cable runs from the bottom cam up to the top where it attaches to the limb tip. When the bowstring is pulled, the cam rotates. The bowstring runs off of the top wheel which bends the bottom limb. The short cable tip, moving away from the axle as the cam turns, bends the top limb. This is a different approach, but one that uses the same principles involved in the two cam bow design.

The difference and real genius built into the *Genesis* bow is that the draw force goes up . . . but never comes down. There is no let-off! It is called a "zero let-off" bow for this reason. But, wait a minute! Isn't let-off that makes compound bows special? Well, yes, but it is also let-off that gives a compound bow it's own draw length. And it

The Genesis *bow goes up to its "peak weight" . . . and stays there (no let-off).*

 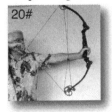 

Here I am with my friend Jeremy proving that big kids and small kids can all shoot the Genesis *bow without making any changes to the bow. A big kid trying to shoot a small kid's "real" compound is going to have trouble.*

requires time and equipment to adjust the bow's draw length to match an archer's draw length. Which is why "regular" compound bows (those with let-off) are almost never used in youth archery programs. (Shooting a "real"

I put some flags on the cables on this Genesis *bow so you could see how they moved during the draw.*

compound when the draw length of the bow doesn't match your draw length is just awful!) With zero let-off, the bow has no fixed draw length built in. Essentially anybody can shoot one without adjusting it (*see the photos*).

On top of all that, you can adjust the *Genesis* bow's draw force from about 15# all of the way up to 20#. All you do is just screw its limb bolts in (more draw weight) or out (less draw weight). But no more than four full turns out from bottom on either bolt! You don't want the limbs to come off!

So, you get to experience shooting a compound bow and get different draw lengths and draw weights built in. This is really cool and why the *Genesis* bow and others of its type ("zero let-off") are really, really popular.

So, why would anybody want a "real" compound? Good question. The highest scores ever shot are by compound archers with the bow's draw length adjusted to exactly match the archers draw length. The bow's draw length being built into the bow actually causes the archer to be more consistent in his draw length. And consistency is absolutely necessary for shooting high scores.

Having said all of this, we don't usually start beginners on compound bows of any kind because they are quite heavy to lift, and relatively expensive. Real compound bows also have those fixed draw lengths that have to be fit to each archer.

When you are selecting compound bows to shoot, here is what we recommend.

Start with a Zero Let-off Bow For the reasons already said, the advantages to starting this way are huge!

Start with the Lowest Draw Weight You Can Use Don't fall into the trap of wanting to brag about pulling the most draw weight. You want to focus on learning to shoot well.

More draw weight will come naturally and in time. Don't make it a roadblock to learning good archery form and execution by trying more than you need.

1001, 1002, 1003 . . .

If The Bow Is Too Heavy, Try Another The test for "too heavy" is if you can lift the bow straight out to your side and count to five . . . slowly . . . then the bow is not too heavy. If you can't get to five . . . slowly . . . then the bow is too heavy (*see photo*).

This bow may be too heavy, it is already starting to drop. You need to be able to count at least to five, slowly, while holding the bow in normal position.

Longbows

Longbows are fun! I love shooting mine. Yes, just like Robin Hood or Legolas! Actually, Legolas was shooting in a "showy" style only good for the movies, no serious archer would shoot that way . . . but his bow was legit. His bow had "ears" on it making it a "static limb tip" bow. These were invented hundreds of years ago to add power to a bow.

The basic idea of a longbow is that the bow is a springy stick that tapers from the handle to each limb tip. This makes the limb tips the easiest part of the bow to bend. As the string is pulled the limb tips bend first then the thicker and thicker parts bend, but less and less as you get closer to the handle. (The part under your hand will bend, too, unless a block of wood is glued there to keep it from bending—the beginning of the "riser!") The ears on Legolas's bow kept the tips from bending, making the thicker parts of the bow bend more, making for a more stout bow.

But I am getting ahead of the story.

A longbow is often described as being a "stick and a string," which it essentially is. The stick is tapered from handle to each tip and at the limb tips, a groove or notch is carved to make sure the

Here I am with a longbow at the 2006 USA Archery Traditional Nationals.

string doesn't slip off. The handle may be bare or wrapped with string or leather strips. The arrow rest . . . is the top knuckle of your bow hand!

That's it! No gewgaws. No arrow rests. No stabilizers. No bow sights. No clickers. Just the bow, the arrow, and you.

And it is truly amazing how well good longbow archers can shoot. I shoot the longbow mostly for fun. (Translation: I don't practice it much.) And even I am amazed at how well I can shoot such bows.

We generally don't start beginners on longbows because longbows designed for beginners and kids are hard to find and are relatively expensive. (This is getting better as more and more young archers embrace "traditional archery.") Longbows are shot much like recurve bows. When you are selecting bows to shoot, here is what we recommend looking for:

About as Tall as You Are Stand the strung longbow on your shoe top. (You never place the tip on the ground.)

38

The other tip should come to somewhere between your chin and your eyes but it can be longer. That is the recommend length.

Start with the Lowest Draw Weight You Can Use When it comes to how much draw weight you want in a bow, less is more. When you are learning how to shoot, if the bow is too hard to pull, you won't be able to use good archery form to draw the bow. This will actually make you a worse archer! Don't fall into the trap of wanting to brag about pulling the stoutest bow in class. Besides, it will just be embarrassing when someone pulling less weight out-shoots you during class! You can use the "Draw Weight Test" described in the recurve bow section to measure how much weight you should be drawing.

Laminated Bows are Safer Robin Hood's bows were made out of one, or occasionally two, pieces of wood. These are called "self bows." They are relatively easy to break. And if you leave them strung for a time, say all day or sometimes just 4-5 hours, they can be "bent" permanently. This drastically lowers the draw weight of the bow. Many modern longbows are made from thin layers of wood (and also fiberglass strips) glued together (much like plywood). These "laminated bows" are much stronger, harder to break, and don't take a permanent bend as easily as do self bows (or ever). Having a bow break while you are shooting is really scary . . . and dangerous . . . so leave off trying a self bow until you are an experienced archer. Go with a laminated longbow.

In Chapter 5 I will go over the details you need to know if you are going to get your own archery equipment. And, you should know that there is a lot more to learn about bows than could be covered here. There are some cool books on bows available. Check the appendices.

In the next chapter we will look at arrows and all of the other stuff you need to be able to use to be a good beginning archer.

Chapter 2 Q & A s

Q My uncle is a bowhunter and he says I can try his bow and arrow. Is this okay?

A Like almost all archers, your uncle wants to encourage young people getting into the sport they so enjoy. Unfortunately, adult equipment is typically too heavy and has too much draw weight for most kids to handle. If it is a compound bow, it probably has too much draw length adjusted in, too. But, the next time you see your uncle, do the "Is the bow too heavy?" test and if it is not, ask him if it is okay to draw the bow. I strongly urge you to only do this if there is an arrow attached and a safe target available. It is really easy (and embarrassing) to dry fire someone else's bow! So, if you can't draw the bow using good form the best reply is to hand the bow back and say "I'm not quite up to this bow yet, but thanks for letting me try."

Going to great lengths to draw a bow you can't handle easily is a big mistake and can only lead to problems. Please do not do this.

Q My archery teacher won't let me try the bows I want to try. What do I say to get him to let me?

A Sorry, if your archery instructor thinks you shouldn't try a particular bow, I have to side with him/her. There are a lot of things involved in making that decision which I didn't go into in this book and I don't know what your situation is. Hey, cut your instructor some slack. If you practice with just the equipment you have available, don't be surprised if he changes his mind in a while and you are allowed to shoot all kinds of bows.

The key thing in my mind is I want all of my students to have really good archery form before we switch to other bows or go up in draw weight. (I start all of my students, even the adults, on a bow with a draw weight of 10 pounds! You might be complaining even more if I were your coach!

Q My big brother has this really cool bow, but he won't let me try it. He isn't being fair!

A You aren't going to win this one. *To be my student, you have to agree to not let anyone else use your equipment!* Here is the reason. Bows and arrows are weapons. If you let someone use yours, and someone is injured, guess who is liable for any accident? You are! And since you are underage, your parents bear all of the responsibility. Your brother is doing the right thing. He may also be a real pain, but that's not my problem as it has nothing to do with archery!

If your brother decides he would like to teach archery to you or anyone else, he just has to be 15 years old and take a course. It is really fun. He can earn money doing it. (And, I will tell you that most young kids prefer having a teenage coach to having an old guy, like me.)

Nock—
Typically made of
plastic, can be
glued on or
pressed into place

Fletching—
Fletches can be
Vanes (plastic) or
Feathers or Mylar
(helium ballon
stuff)

Shaft—
May be made of
aluminum (like this
one) or fiberglass,
or carbon fiber, or
wood. All but wood
shafts are hollow.

Point—
made of steel,
may be sharp or dull

Chapter 3
Arrows and
A Lot More

Bows are cool! Bows are available in hot colors. Arrows are . . . kinda dull. But guess which is more important for accurate archery?

Is it the bow?

Or is it the arrows?

Uh huh, it is the arrows. Obviously we want both bow and arrows to be good. But an expert archer with an iffy bow and good arrows will always outshoot another expert archer with super bow and iffy arrows.

Let's look at arrows. And then we will look at some of the other equipment that can get involved.

Arrows

Arrows are all the same and they are all different. They are all the same in that they all have a shaft, a nock, a point, and fletches.

There are all different in that they all have different lengths, weights, diameters, kinds of fletches, etc. The most important difference is what they are made of.

As target archers, we want every one of our arrows to be as identical to the others as we can make them. Having

43

our arrows all different would make archery really difficult. So, we have to choose what kind of arrows to shoot. Then we have to choose the right size, then the right points and fletches, etc. When taking lessons with borrowed or program equipment the choices are made for you. To decide what you might want to buy, look in Chapter 5. Here we are going to focus on just the kinds of arrows that show up in beginning classes.

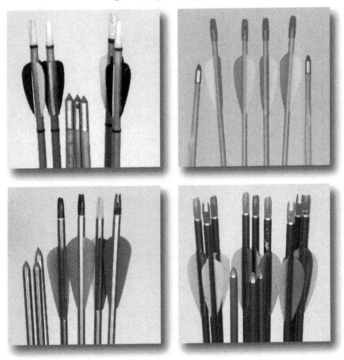

All modern arrows are tubes. They are hollow. Well, hollow with one exception: wood arrows. Wooden arrows are solid wood. Robin Hood shot with wood arrows as did everyone up to about 70 years ago. We do not recommend wood arrows even if you decide you want to shoot a longbow, like Robin Hood. Wood arrows break fairly easily and the pieces are sharp enough to cut you. So, if you want to shoot traditionally, with a longbow and wood arrows, we recommend you learn on more durable arrows and only take up wood when you are an accomplished archer.

The materials beginner arrows are made of are: fiberglass, aluminum, and carbon fiber (*see the photos left*).

Fiberglass Arrows Fiberglass arrows (*upper right*) tend to last a long time but are kind of heavy. Heavy arrows can't be shot as far as light ones. The shafts are made of glass fibers embedded in plastic. They are really hard to repair. But they are inexpensive. We don't use these in our programs but some programs do. (*The photo shows what happens when they break: they create a lot of really sharp fibers, so dispose of these carefully.*)

Aluminum Arrows These arrows have shafts which are aluminum metal tubes, like long drinking straws. (It's the same high-quality aluminum they make airplanes out of.) They are durable and easy to repair. They are more expensive than fiberglass arrows but not a lot so. Aluminum arrows are lightweight but they can be bent. It is easy enough to straighten them, but you really don't want to shoot arrows once they get bent, so you have to watch out.

Carbon Arrows Carbon arrows (*lower right*) are like fiberglass arrows. The shafts are made of carbon fibers embedded in plastic (like golf club shafts). This makes them the most expensive arrows, but they are also the lightest and they do not bend. They are also quite hard to break, but when they do they break like fiberglass arrows so dispose of them properly.

Your program may use any of these kinds of arrows.

What to Watch For

If you have fiberglass arrows (they tend to be pale yellow or black in color), you just want to make sure that all of the parts are there. The most dangerous thing that can happen is to have a cracked arrow nock. (The nock is the part that snaps onto the string.) If you think a nock is cracked, ask your instructor to check it. If a single fletch is lost, the arrow can still be shot. If two fletches are lost, the arrow should not be shot.

If you have aluminum arrows (the shiny ones) you have to add "don't shoot them if they are bent" to the list of things to look for. If you have an arrow that looks bent, ask your instructor to check it.

If you have carbon arrows (they are almost always black) you don't have to worry about them being bent. You do have to watch for cracks. Add "don't shoot them if they are cracked" to the list of things to look for. If you think an arrow is cracked, ask your instructor to check it.

The most dangerous thing about any arrow is if it is too short. Too short arrows can fall off of the bow when the string is pulled and land on the back of your hand (*see photos below*). Your instructor/coach should check your arrow's length before you are assigned to use them.

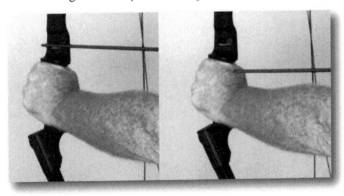

If you accidently pull an arrow off the bow onto your hand, *do not let go of the string*. Ask for help if you need it to execute a let down safely. Then ask your instructor why that happened.

The Lot More

There are quite a few other things involved in beginning archery. Some come sooner, others later. I am going to lump them into three categories: Things You Can Put On a Bow, Things You Wear, and Other Things.

Things You Can Put On a Bow

There are a great many things you can attach to your bow for any number of reasons.

(best for now)

Arrow Rests Arrow rests are simple to complex and can be inexpensive (<$3) to really expensive (well over $100). They can be glued or screwed onto the bow or bolted on. There are hundreds of different models available.

(for Olympic recurve)

(for compound with release aid)

Their job is to provide a stable position from which your arrows are launched.

Stabilizers Stabilizers are just rods screwed into holes provided in your bow's riser. They make a bow easier to hold steady. Lately they also absorb the vibrations left over after shots, so they don't make you tired. (If you don't think vibrations make you tired, ask the construction guys who operate jack hammers!)

Photo Courtesy of Dean Alberge

Modern stabilizers almost all absorb vibrations left over after shots are made. The vibrations not absorbed can get absorbed by you and will make you tired. (Just ask any guy whose job it is to operate a jackhammer!)

Photo Courtesy of Lloyd Brown

Clickers Clickers are little springy blades that you attach so they can ride along the top of your arrow as it is drawn. When you draw the bow, the arrows slides under the clicker which falls off the tip when you are at full draw (and goes "click"). This tells you when you have drawn the bow as far as you did the last time. All Olympic archers

48

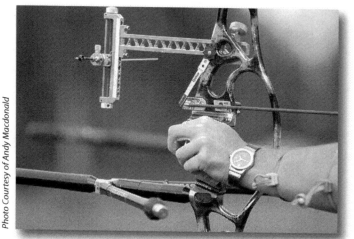

Photo Courtesy of Andy Macdonald

Clickers come in many forms: some are magnetic, others just springy. Many beginners have their clicker attached to their sight's extension bar to allow for longer arrows. They all work the same way, though: they are placed on top of the arrow and when the arrow slides back, they fall off and "click."

use clickers. Most other archers do not.

Things You Wear

The most common things archers wear are armguards, finger tabs, quivers, chest protectors, and hats.

Armguards There are dozens of different styles of armguards. My rule is simple regarding them: if you are a beginner, you must wear an armguard. Getting hit by a bowstring is like being whipped. It really, really hurts. Why take the chance by not wearing one?

If you look around, you will see many adults not wearing armguards. Usually these are compound bow archers. The way a compound bow is shot makes hitting your arm much less likely (at least once you have learned how). If you shoot a compound and when you are no longer a beginner, you can take yours off. Or leave it on,

All recurve and longbow archers wear an armguard (see photos previous pages). *Most compound archers do not, although there are exceptions (most notably Jaime Van Natta* (upper right) *who is probably the best female compound archer in the world right now). Not using an armguard often leads to bruised arms.* (Photos Courtesy of Lloyd Brown)

many champions do!

Tabs There are dozens of different styles of finger tabs. Cheap tabs cause more trouble than they prevent. For the same reasons we do not recommend shooting gloves to beginners either (*see photos*). Tabs must be properly fit to an archer to work well. My rule is that beginners can skip using a finger tab unless their fingers start to get sore. Your coach/instructor may require them.

Quivers Like most other things there are a lot of

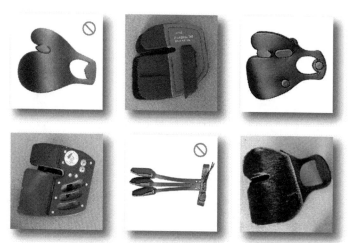

"wearable" quiver choices. There are hip quivers, back quivers, pocket quivers, etc (*see photos below*). Most recreational archers start using ground quivers, so there is nothing to wear. The next step is usually to a hip quiver. The most useful ones have multiple pockets or tubes to keep arrows in and a pouch or pouches to keep tools, pencils (to keep score), tabs, arrow pullers, etc.

51

Bowhunters like quivers that bolt onto their bows but target archers do not use these as they change the balance of their bows as the arrows are removed.

Chest Protectors These are also called "string guards" and other things (*see photos below*). Only Olympic-style archers tend to wear these. What they do is prevent your bowstring from catching on your clothing. If you want to shoot Olympic-style, you will probably end up wearing one. Be aware that they are notorious for fitting poorly. It is not only okay, but probably mandatory, that you adjust their shape with pins or paper clips or needle and thread so that they fit better.

Hats "I gotta wear a hat?" Well, no, you can just let the hot sun bake your brains out! Hats keep the sun out of your eyes while aiming and keep your head cool (*see photos on page 54*). Archers wear them even indoors because there are many lights indoors to get in your eyes. Lots of archers wear baseball caps, but recurve archers usually do not. This is because the bill of a baseball cap often ends up touching the bowstring of a recurve bow at full draw.

Mechanical Release Aids

"Release Aids" are mechanical triggers that can be used to draw and release the bowstring, usually better than you can with just your fingers. They are not allowed in Olympic, traditional, and even some compound shooting styles. They are very popular with bowhunters and the top "unlimited" compound target archers. There are two basic types: wriststrap releases and hand-held releases.

Both of these kinds cost from $100-$300 for a really good one and it must be sized to fit you. There are hundreds of different models available.

Learning to shoot arrows with good form is difficult. I recommend that you learn to shoot with your fingers on the string first. Then you can add stabilizers and bow sights (if you want). Near the end, after you have learned to shoot, I teach you how to shoot with a release aid. Trying to learn how to shoot with all the gewgaws in place from the beginning is really hard. Some have done it, but I don't recommend it.

Other Things There are a great many other things that archers like to have while shooting (*see the sidebar "Mechanical Release Aids"*). To keep this simple I am going to limit this part to just "archery tools." The most common tools archers have with them are Allen wrenches, arrow pullers, a bow square, and small adjustable wrenches (*see photo at right*). The Allen wrenches are needed because almost all of the screws in a bow are screws that need an Allen wrench to tighten or loosen.

Obviously if you have a longbow, you won't need wrenches, screwdrivers, or any tools at all. (Robin Hood didn't need them!) Compound archers need more tools because their bows have more parts.

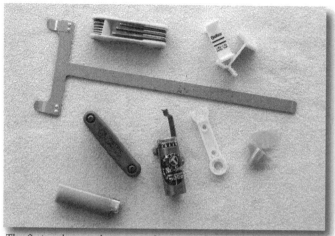

The first archery tool most people get is a "bow square" (it's the long thingy), next is a set of Allen wrenches (US sizes in yellow, metric in red).

Chapter 3 Q & A s

Q My cousin has some archery equipment she will give me. Can I have the arrows cut down to fit me?

A This sounds like a good idea but it doesn't work. The arrow you need to shoot is based on how much draw weight and draw length you have. Beginners, especially kids, have short draw lengths and low draw weights. This means they need arrows that are not very stiff. Adults, with longer draw lengths and higher draw weights need stiffer arrows. So, your cousin's arrows are probably too long and too stiff for you. If you cut them down a bit, they will be shorter (good!) but that also makes them way stiffer (very bad!). There is no way to make arrows much less stiff.

If your cousin really wants to give you the equipment, it is okay to take it. If you don't "grow into it," you might be able to trade it for equipment you can use. Either would make your cousin happy, we guess.

Q A friend of mine says he can shoot an arrow with no feathers on it. He is kidding me, isn't he?

A Actually, you can do such a thing, too. An arrow with no fletching is called a "bare shaft." These things are used to "tune" your bow and arrows. The fletches, feathers or plastic, act somewhat like airplane wings and straighten the flight of arrows that are launched a little funny. As long as you shoot really well, and don't launch arrows at odd angles, a bare shaft will fly much like an ordinary arrow.

I don't recommend you try shooting bare shafts until you become at least an intermediate archer. (A badly shot bare shaft often ends up broken.)

Q I've seen these really cool quivers that have your name on them and everything. Should I get one?

A Those quivers are cool . . . and they cost $180-200 or more. I am not going to tell you you shouldn't get such things as I have a quiver that costs close to that much. But, they don't help you shoot any better. I think you ought to spend your money on things that help you to become a better archer first. Save the "flashy" things as rewards for winning a competition or achieving some other milestone.

Q I want to win an Olympic medal, should I be using a clicker?

A Eventually, yes. But I don't start students on using clickers (or metal arrow rests, etc.) until they have their own bow and arrows. And they need good archery form.

They especially need to have a consistent draw length. Clickers have to be set up carefully. Clickers have to be learned. You need to work with an experienced archery coach when you take on a clicker.

Q I saw a picture of an archer who had a long rod-like thing with a weight on the end. Do I need one of those?

A That stabilizer (*see photo*) is called a "long rod" or a "long stabilizer." Weights are placed on the tip, the middle, and at the base to bal-

ance the bow. The balance needed is for the bow to slowly "bow" toward the target after the shot. The first stabilizer I suggest you try is a relatively short (24-30″) long rod with no end weight. The stabilizer itself makes the bow heavier and harder to hold up. Get used to the weight of the bow with the rod first. Then longer rods or stabilizer weights can be tried once you are used to it.

Q Do I have to use a finger tab? They are so clunky!

A The problem with most "beginner tabs" is that the word "beginner" just means "cheap." Cheap tabs are no use to anyone and just get in the way. A properly fitting tab helps two ways: it protects your fingers and it makes it easier for the bowstring to slide off of your fingers. If you want to buy a personal tab, see Chapter 5 for my recommendation.

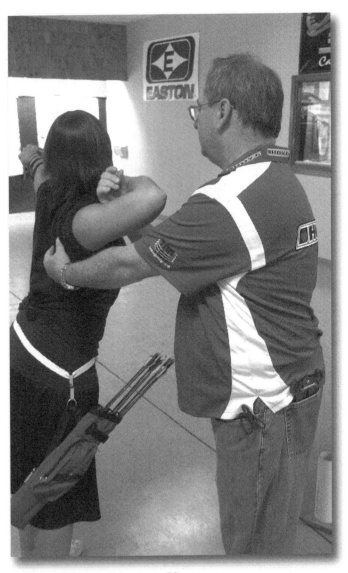

Chapter 4
Shooting

I've seen it happen over and over: an eight-year old who really wants to try archery steps up to the shooting line for his first shot. Convinced this is going to be hard, the little soon-to-be archer flexes every muscle he has and thereby cannot move at all, let alone pull the bowstring. (Try it! Flex all of your muscles and you can't move!) He just stands there, bow in hand, quivering, with nothing happening. When I convince him that it is important to relax, he then gets that first arrow off.

Much less than an hour later he is shooting independently and having a ball.

But, after that, he asks "Now what do I do?"

That's a good question. Let's talk about shooting.

The Framework of a Shot

After learning to relax so as to be able to shoot at all (Lesson #1), what is the next thing to learn? Actually, you don't have to do anything else. You can just let the bow and arrow teach you. Just keep shooting and you'll figure out most of what you need to do. The process is called "trial and error" and it can be used to learn almost anything. But progress is often slow and frustrating. There are ways to learn to shoot better more quickly.

59

Does this sound good to you? If so, continue reading.

The first step in really learning how to shoot well is to look at all of the parts of a shot.

"Parts? You mean like Step #1 Pull Back, Step #2 Let go?" you ask?

Exactly! These two steps constitute what is called a *shot sequence* or *shot routine*. The number of steps can be as little as two or it can be over twenty. Since an archery shot is one consistent motion, it can have as many parts as we want.

The idea of breaking a shot down into parts does two things: it gives you and people like me (coaches) a common set of parts to discuss. It also allows you to look just at the "parts" that are weak, so you can practice them and "get better." (Our goal is to always have all of the "parts" at the same level of quality.)

Before we look at what parts we want in our sequence, we need to know what "getting better" means. (Hah, and you thought you knew!)

How to Know When You Are "Getting Better" at Archery

You probably think "more bulls-eyes" is the definition of getting better. Let's look at that. Let's say you took three shots at a typical 10 ring target. (The middle ring is worth 10, the outer ring is worth 1.) Which would you prefer— a three arrow score of 10-10-1 or 8-8-8? (Hint: Do the math!)

Yep, the three 8's are worth 24 points, three more than the other set even though it had two bulls-eyes. So, is "more bulls-eyes" the best definition of "getting better?" Well, they do count for the maximum score, but, um, no: "more bulls-eyes" is not the best definition of getting better.

60

The best indicator of "getting better" is based on group size. When our arrows cluster into smaller groups, we are shooting well. When our groups get bigger, we are shooting worse. Look at the diagram. A target with three 8's in it can look like the target in the middle in the diagram or like the target at the right. Which do you think is better?

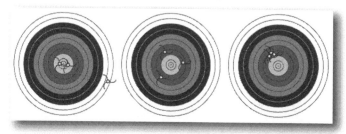

The target on the far right is better because those three arrows were more consistently shot, making a small group. If those three arrows were aimed better, all of them would fit into the 10-ring for a score of 10-10-10. The large group of three 8's won't fit into the ten or even the nine ring, so it can't be just moved for a maximum score. So, smaller groups is always what we are looking for. If the group, like the one in the right target, isn't where we want it, we can move it. But if we can't shoot three arrows pretty much the same way, they won't land close enough together to get that 10-10-10 score. So . . . , *shooting smaller groups is the best indicator of "getting better."*

The only other thing you need to know is that the "normal" sizes of groups changes with distance. If you can shoot three arrows (the minimum to make a group) into a 9″ circle at ten yards, you should be able to shoot three arrows into an 18″ circle at 20 yards. At 30 yards you should be able to group your arrows in a 27″ circle. Two times as far means two times as big a circle, three times as far means three times as big a circle, etc. These "group sizes" are averages. Some days your groups are smaller, sometimes bigger. The more expert you become, the smaller and more consistent your groups become, but nobody is exactly the same day after day.

A Beginner's Shot Sequence

Now that we know how to figure out whether we are doing better (or not), I am going to give you your first shot sequence. As you learn, you may add steps or take away steps. There is no "correct" number of steps. Champion archers have had sequences of four steps and sequences of fourteen steps. If another archer wants to argue with you about what the correct number of steps in a shot sequence is, just smile and walk away. You don't want to get into an argument with an idiot!

The correct number of steps is the number *you* need. If there is part of your shot you want to talk about or work on and it doesn't correspond to one of your steps, make a place for a new step where doing that thing is "the new step." Ta da!

Here's the first sequence I give to my students who are starting to get serious about archery. It is called "The Nine Step to the Ten Ring." And, no, I didn't invent it. I'm not really sure who did.

The Nine Steps to the Ten Ring

This applies to shooting a bow with your fingers on the string.
1. Take Your Stance
2. Nock an Arrow
3. Set Your Hands
4. Raise the Bow

5. Draw
6. Find Your Anchor
7. Aim
8. Release the String
9. Follow Through

This list uses short phrases (the words people use does vary) that summarize what is being done. But, if you don't like any of these, you are free to make up your own lists and your own names for your steps.

Starting on the next page are descriptions of what these are referring to. These are essentially directions as to how to shoot.

1

"take your stance"

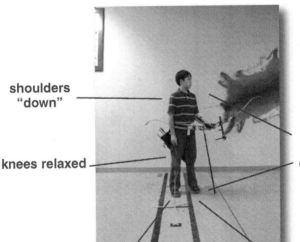

shoulders "down"

knees relaxed

feet, knees, hips, shoulders aligned

feet shoulder width apart

toes on line to target

(Note—this archer uses an "open" stance with his toes on a line pointing to the left of the target)

"nock an arrow"

"see" the arrow below the top nock locator

"hear" the snap onto the string

"see" the index fletch stick out from the bow

(later, maybe) "see" the clicker on top of the arrow

2

3

(Note—later you will have one finger over the arrow and two below— the "split" finger grip of the string)

curl three fingers around the string, under the nock

slide the hand, palm down, into the pivot point

relax the hand and arm

drop the wrist until the bow rests on the pad of the thumb (only)

"set your hands"

keep both
shoulders
"down"

draw wrist is
relaxed

draw elbow
should be
"high"

if using a sight,
raise bow so
you are aiming
above the cen-
ter of the target

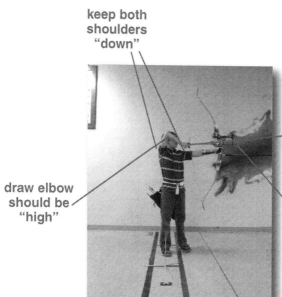

4 "raise the bow"

5

"draw"

If clicker is used, draw ends when clicker is "hanging on the point"

shoulders "down"

draw is smooth and strong

feel tension growing between your shoulder blades

(Note—this archer uses an "low" anchor which is beneath the chin rather than a "high" anchor at the corner of the mouth)

"find your anchor"

"see" the string in the aiming eye (it is very fuzzy)

(low anchor) string at corner of chin, press up

(high anchor) finger in corner of mouth, top finger wrapped around cheek bone, press in

feel tension growing between your shoulder blades

6

7

line up sight
aperture or
arrow point
with your point
of aim

relax

feel tension
growing
between your
shoulder
blades

"aim"

keep both
shoulders
"down"

bow arm
stays still

draw hand
slides back
along face
(this is a
"reaction,"
not an
"action")

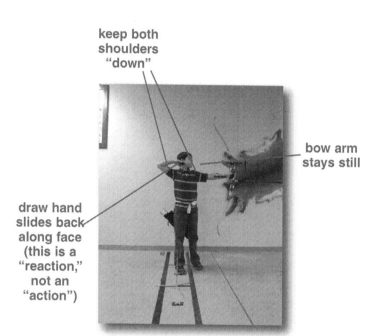

8

"release the string"

"follow through"

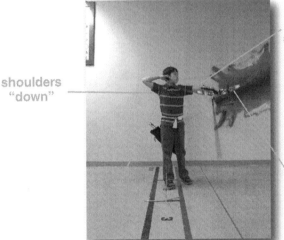

bow arm
stays still

shoulders
"down"

bow rocks
forward

feel tension
growing
between your
shoulder
blades until
bow com-
pletes its
"bow"

(Note—this archer
uses a stabilizer
and the bow
"bows" forward—
if no stabilizer, it
"bows" back—in
either case the
shot is not over
until the bow
"bows")

Some Fine Points of Shooting

- It is key that any muscle not being used stay relaxed.
- The primary muscles used to draw the bow are the muscles used squeeze the shoulder blades (code name: *scapulae*) together.
- The shoulders must be kept as low as possible
- The draw elbow must be kept high (otherwise your brain will use your arm (weak) instead of your back (strong) to draw the bow).
- Keeping the shoulders low while the draw elbow is high is not easy, it takes attention and practice.
- The "release" is not something you do; it occurs when you stop holding onto the string (a relaxation of the muscles in your forearm causes this).
- Even though the bowstring is fuzzy when you are at full draw, you still want to be able to "see" it.
- It is vital that you focus on what you are doing "now" through the entire shot.
- The followthrough is largely a "reaction," not an "action" (other than trying to hold your bow arm up).
- If anything—mental or physical, anything at all—intrudes from a prior step or from outside the shot, you must let down and start over.
- All shot sequences are based upon the fact that for 5-10 seconds (the time it takes to make a shot), you can "set" a body position and it won't change as your focus moves away. This does take training and time to perfect, though.
- The hardest step for beginners? Nocking an arrow. (Hands down!)
- The hardest step for advanced archers? The release, because it requires everything that came before it to be done correctly and after the release, most things happen by themselves.

It is up to you to learn to do these steps consistently.

When you are first learning these it is important to do each step separately. The steps go one . . . **two** . . . three . . . etc. Expert archers run all these together: one**two**three-**four**five, etc. They even overlap steps: one**two**three-**fofui**rve, etc. But it is important you do these steps at least somewhat separately at the start because there is more to learn about each of these steps. In each of the steps there are mental checks to do ("When I attached the arrow did the nock click?" "Is the index vane sticking away from the bow?" "Is the arrow sitting on the arrow rest?" "Has the clicker been slid on top of the arrow?") and these mental steps are part of what is called your "mental program." It is a mental program that allows you to shoot your 30th arrow as well as your fifth. If you start out running all of the steps together, they won't be separate in your mind and you will get mixed up. And when you get mixed up is when you shoot goofy arrows for bad scores. (Me, too; everybody shoots poorly scoring arrows when they get mixed up.)

The Most Important Rule of All

Do you want me to tell you the rule that results in getting better the fastest you can? (Yeah, like you are going to say "no" and toss the book away!)

The rule that gives you the most progress the fastest . . . you'll have to buy my next book . . . no, no, I won't do that to you. Here is the rule. I call it the *Rule of Discipline*: *If anything—mental or physical, anything at all—intrudes from a prior step or from outside the shot, you must let down and start over.*

It is that simple. It is that hard. *All you have to do is not do things wrong.* If you even think you might shoot a wrong shot, start over. Every time you shoot a shot you know isn't being done the right way, you are giving yourself permission to do it again (and again, and again, and . . .). Such shots usually do not score well. You only want to shoot shots that are shot right. You certainly don't want to practice making wrong shots!

If you get a chance to watch professional archers shoot (for real or on video—just search for "archery" on YouTube, for examples) you will see them make "let downs." Often when they do a let down they will take the arrow off of their bow and start the shot over . . . from the beginning. They are following the *Rule of Discipline.* All of the top archers do this.

Chapter 5 Q & A s

Q My friend got a new bow and he says he shoots a whole bunch better. Will that work for me?

A Sometimes it will. If your "old bow" is the wrong size, wrong weight, or wrong draw weight and the new bow gets all of these things right, it will definitely improve your scores. But realize that the top archers are at the top year after year after year. And each year their bow sponsor gives them a new bow. So, is it the bow or the archer?

It's the archer. (Same archer, different bows, still wins consistently.) This has been proven over and over.

Hey, I like getting new gear, but the only time new gear makes things better is when my old gear was somehow limiting my performance. That doesn't happen too often. (I still like new stuff, I just don't expect it to make me better.) Practice can make you better a lot cheaper. (And I know you didn't want to hear this.)

Q I heard of a baseball player who uses a sports psychologist, do archers do that?

A Some have, but most don't. All of the top target archers, though, are really aware of the way their minds work and always have a set of "mental tools" to use while shooting. Just, like baseball players and golfers, though, when the pressure of competition gets cranked up, sometimes the advice of a good sports psychologist can help. I have never met a beginning archer who has consulted a sport psychologist, but, hey, if it is your Mom or Dad, it can't hurt!

Q My friend says that aiming is the most important thing? Is that true?

A I am going to have to disagree. To me the most important thing is to be focussing on what you are doing while you are doing it. If you are focussing on aiming and you are just getting ready to load an arrow on your bow, this is not good. When you are aiming, aiming is the most important thing. Otherwise, not.

Q My sister says that splitting an arrow with another arrow is just a special effect seen in the movies? Can it be done?

A Yep. Since modern arrows are tubes, the arrows don't split so much that one slides into the other. This is still called a "Robin Hood" by many (also "tubing" or "telescoping" an arrow). I have reputable reports of archers who have shot one arrow that "split" a previous arrow and then did the same thing to the second arrow—a double Robin Hood! There is also a reputable story about a guy who "called his shot," that is announced he was going to Robin Hood an arrow and then did it!

I don't recommend you do this though, it gets really expensive! (Although there is an unwritten rule in NFAA competition, that if you "tube" another archer's arrow, you get to keep it as a trophy.)

The reason it looks like a forest of bows is because there really are so many to choose from! And these are just compound and recurve target bows; there are thousands more of other varieties.

Chapter 5
Getting
Your Own Gear!

"When should I get my own bow and arrow?" you ask.

Good question! The answer is "any time." But—you knew there was going to be a "but," didn't you?—*you need to know how to shoot fairly well to get your money's worth.* For example, it is not uncommon for your draw length to change quite a bit while you are first learning what good archery form is. Also, the draw weight you can handle goes up as you learn and practice. If you buy before these things settle in, you may being going right back to the store to get new equipment that fits the "new you" real soon.

Many people get started with borrowed equipment (I did!). Or you can start by buying new or even used equipment. In all of these cases, here are my general guidelines.

1. *Don't buy really expensive gear at first.* Some coaches suggest that you really need the "best" equipment if you want to make progress. I not only don't agree, I vehemently disagree. (And, trust me, I can really vehement!) Some of the most expensive bows and arrows are very "touchy" to shoot and can only be handled by experts. What you really need is equipment capable of

shooting better than you can. (This rule always applies.) As a beginner, solid equipment can be had for not much money.

2. *Don't buy really cheap equipment (ever).* Cheap equipment breaks. Cheap equipment doesn't work right. Don't waste your time or money on cheap equipment. By "cheap" I don't mean inexpensive. I mean stay away from "archery sets" sold in big sporting goods stores, that kind of thing. I often buy used equipment. Top of the line equipment of five years ago is really good stuff, it just isn't "new" and it is way less expensive than brand new stuff. And it is definitely not "cheap." (Buying "used" requires you to have or get expert advice.)

3. *It always pays to get help.* I provide a service to my students called a "Bow Fitting" which is just going through all of the steps necessary to fit archery equipment to you. In the end I give them a shopping list with everything they need on it, along with one or two recommendations per item as to manufacturer and cost. If your coach/instructor can't do this for you, a good archery shop can. Be aware that most archery shops are set up to serve mostly bowhunters and not young target archers, so don't expect miracles from a shop. If you have a good archery shop nearby, you have been blessed, so appreciate them!

4. *It is always wise to "try before you buy."* At a bare minimum you would like to try the equipment in the shop selling it to you before you buy it. Often, people will lend you pieces of equipment for you to try out to see if you like it enough to get your own. A "try" usually takes several days, but even a short "try" is better than nothing. Don't try out something and say "I don't like this" five minutes later. Every time you try something

new it feels awkward for the first 3-4 times you use it. You have to keep trying it until the "awkward" wears off. Then you can decide whether it works or not.

Getting a Bow

First you have to decide what kind of bow you want: recurve bow, compound bow, or longbow. Then you have to decide what size and how much draw weight. You will probably have a "budget" to keep in mind also. A great help are online archery store catalogs. I recommend Lancaster Archery Supply (*www.lancasterarchery.com*). Also, there is Alternative Sporting Services (really unfortunate initials, but a good company) in England (*www.altservices.co.uk*). You can look up "Youth Recurve Bows" or "Youth Compound Bows" quite easily. While they don't carry every model of bow made, they do carry a lot of them, as well as a boatload of other target archery stuff.

You can also get an idea of what a "good" price is from these online retailers (not "great" but "good"). If you have a local archery shop, please realize that they may not have as good of a price. But also realize that your shop is giving you service with your purchase that you don't get online. An archery shop will set the bow up for you (adjust it, etc.) and, if anything goes wrong, they will make it right. Certainly those are reasons to shop locally. On the other hand, if the shop's prices are way higher, maybe buying online isn't so bad.

Here's my advice for when you are bow shopping.

Recurve Bows for Beginners

In general three-piece bows (top limb + handle + bottom limb = 3 pieces) are recommended because if you want to change draw weight or bow length, often you only need to purchase a new set of limbs to attach to the handle. Consequently I am supplying "good" prices for both bows and limbs.

Also, you must check to see if the bow comes with a bowstring and an arrow rest. If not, purchase an inexpensive "Fast Flight" bowstring the same length as your bow (a 66″ bow takes a 66″ string—it isn't 66″ long, just designed for that length bow—about $10) and/or purchase a Hoyt *Super Hunter* stick-on arrow rest ($2.95) or a plastic screw-in rest ($2.95).

All prices are considered "good" (as of 2010) and, of course, will vary from place to place.

Wooden Handled Three Piece Recurve Bows
Bow $80 (48″) to $110 (66″)
Pair of Limbs $42 (48″) to $55 (66″)
Polymer Handled Three Piece Recurve Bow
Bow $120 (64″ to 66″)
Pair of Limbs $55
Metal Handled Three Piece Recurve Bow
Bow $160-200 (64″ to 68″)
Pair of Limbs $80-100

The metal risered bows typically have "adjustable limb pockets" that allow you to reduce the draw weight of a pair of limbs by about 10%. This means you have to change limbs only about half as often, so this proves to be an economical choice over the long term.

All of these bows are good. If you have a really damp climate, consider the polymer (plastic) handled bows as they don't swell or warp like wood or corrode (rust) like metal.

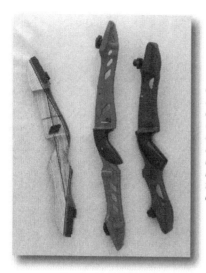

The "riser" or "handle" of a three piece recurve bow may be made out of wood (left), metal (center), or polymer (plastic, right). All can be painted, but typically the wood risers only have a clear finish and the polymer risers have color blended in.

Compound Bows for Beginners

In general, most compound bows are designed for hunters, which usually makes them unsuitable for target archery. Most manufacturers, though, tend to make a number of very good "youth bows."

Recommendations Specific to Youth Compounds Other than the *Genesis* bow, there are a number of other zero-let-off bows for about $200-250. If you are serious, though, you will want a bow with let-off. These are usually labeled as "youth compound bows." In the youth compound bow market, for $275-390, I would look for:

Draw Weight	a maximum of 40#, 30-35# is better
Draw Length	adjustable for several inches (typically 18-26″ or so)
Axle-to-Axle Length	no less than 35″ (You may have to compromise on this.)
Let-off	50-65% (no more)

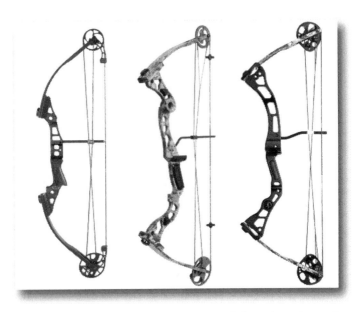

Since these bows have a range of draw lengths and draw weights, and since these are both likely to go up as you grow and practice, try to get a bow where you are near the lower end of these ranges. Otherwise, you could end up having to buy another bow relatively quickly as you run out of draw length or draw weight.

Short length bows (<35″ axle-to-axle) are very hard to shoot with a tab unless the draw weight is really low (<25#). This is why I recommend a longer bow to you.

Compound bows tend to be physically quite heavy, so you do not want to load them up with accessories (bow sight, stabilizer, etc.) at the start. Shoot the thing barebow until you get used to the weight. Then you can add stuff.

Oh, after you sort through all of the stuff above, then you can choose whatever color you like. Early on Claudia had a young student who went shopping with his Mom and a shopping list we gave him. He came back with a bow that was too large, too heavy, and too hard to draw. But it was red . . . and it had decorative flames! C'mon now, a "pretty" bow is one that shoots good! An "ugly" bow is one you can't handle. I don't care what color they are. If you do, make it the last thing to add to your decision of which bow to buy.

The shop and/or your coach will be able to adjust the bow's draw length to match your draw length and set your draw weight up to be comfortable.

Longbows for Beginners

There are not a great many longbows made for youths (more are being made with time, thankfully). I recommend that you measure from your shoe top to your nose as a good estimate of how long a bow you can use. (If you are still growing or expect to grow a lot, you can add 4-6 inches to this length.) I recommend you get a laminated bow with "a shelf." The "shelf" is a ledge cut into the bow's han-

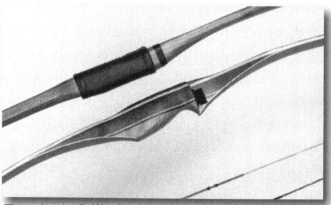

The top bow is a "self bow" and the "layers" you can see are just the natural grain of the wood. The bottom bow has laminations of dark and light woods and a shelf built in to be used as an arrow rest.

dle that acts as an arrow rest. The draw weight of this bow should be the same as described above for recurve bows.

Getting Arrows

In general, most beginners are better off with aluminum arrows. They combine the best of affordability, shootability, and durability. Recommended point weight is about 50-80 grains (NIBB points if you can get them, bullet points if not) fletched with 2-2.5″ plastic vanes. You can buy half of a dozen to see how well they work, then go back for more. It is important that you realize that as you grow you will need different arrows, usually longer and stiffer. For this reason alone, we don't recommend you invest in really good arrows (*aka* "expensive arrows") until much later.

Specific Arrow Recommendations Here are my recommendations for arrows. There are lots of arrows available for young people, so you don't have to stick with just these. Your local shop may have a killer sale on better arrows for less money. Keep your eyes open.

Easton Jazz Arrows
This is *the* entry-level aluminum arrow!
(~$45 per dozen—more if with NIBB points)

Easton Platinum Plus
These arrows are one step up in quality from
Jazz arrows. The main difference is the nocks
are "press in" rather than "glue on" which makes them
easier to adjust and to replace.
(~$65 per dozen—more if with NIBB points))

We usually recommend NIBB points or bullet points in your arrows, even though they are more expensive. The cheapest arrow points (There's that word "cheap" again.) tend to rust, break and pop out more often. Bullet points (better) and NIBB points (best) don't rust as easily, protect the arrows from bending better, and don't pop out as easily.

Fitting Arrows Arrows have to be "fit" to an archer's skill and an archer's bow. This is done by buying arrows with the correct spine and cutting them to the correct length. (Spine roughly corresponds to the arrow's stiffness or resilience.) The trouble is that the arrow's length is matched to an archer's measured draw length, but beginner's draw lengths are volatile and can change one to two inches as their form matures. If your draw length goes down, there is no problem. If it goes up, arrows can become too short and therefore become unshootable. To avoid this problem, always order arrows for beginners *uncut.* But longer arrows are less stiff than shorter ones, so to correct for this, use this rule of thumb: for every extra inch of arrow, use one spine group stiffer shafts. So, if the "uncut" shaft is three inches longer than an archer's draw length, you would move three spine groups stiffer on the arrow manufacturer's spine chart.

What is a spine chart? It is a chart of arrow lengths matched against bow draw weights with the manufacturer's recommendation(s) for each combination (*see next page for an example*). For Easton's spine chart, go to: *www.eastonarchery.com*, click on "Downloads" and "Target Selection Chart." (Every arrow manufacturer has their own spine chart.)

This is a task that a good shop or good coach will shine at. Getting help here is really important. Also, aluminum arrows do get bent. Often coaches can straighten

This is the 2009 Easton Target Archery Spine Chart (top). To use it, you select your draw weight (for compound bows, the left three columns, depending on the kind of cams—for recurve bows from the rightmost column). Then you slide across your row until you get to your draw length. There are 14 spine groups showing and, unfortunately, the information you need as a youth beginner may be off of the chart! (Luckily they made a chart just for youths (see right)!) We recommend that you get your arrows uncut, which requires them to be in one spine group stiffer (upward) for every inch longer than your actual draw length.

88

Correct Arrow Length for Youth Target

20½ (52.1 cm) 21" 21½ (54.6 cm)	21½ (54.6 cm) 22" 22½ (57.2 cm)	22½ (57.2 cm) 23" 23½ (59.7 cm)	23½ (59.7 cm) 24" 24½ (62.2 cm)	24½ (62.2 cm) 25" 25½ (64.8 cm)	25½ (64.8 cm) 26" 26½ (67.3 cm)	26½ (67.3 cm) 27" 27½ (69.9 cm)	RECURVE BOW Bow Weight - lbs. Finger Release
		Y1	Y1	Y2	Y3	Y4	16-20 lbs. (7.3-9.1 kg)
	Y1	Y1	Y2	Y3	Y4	Y5	20-24 lbs. (9.1-10.9 kg)
Y1	Y1	Y2	Y3	Y4	Y5	Y6	24-28 lbs. (10.9-12.7 kg)
Y1	Y2	Y3	Y4	Y5	Y6	Y7	28-32 lbs. (12.7-14.5 kg)
Y2	Y3	Y4	Y5	Y6	Y7		32-36 lbs. (14.5-16.3 kg)
Y3	Y4	Y5	Y6	Y7			36-40 lbs. (16.3-18.1 kg)

Size	Spine	Model	Weight Grs/Inch	Wt @29"	Size	Spine	Model	Weight Grs/Inch	Wt @29"
Group Y1					**Group Y2**				
1214	2.501	75	5.9	171	1413	2.036	75	5.9	171
Group Y3					**Group Y4**				
1413	2.036	75	5.9	171	2-00	1.530	A/C/C	4.7	136
1416	1.684	75	7.2	209	1416	1.684	75	7.2	209
Group Y5					**Group Y6**				
1250	1.250	A/C/E	5.1	148	1250	1.250	A/C/E	5.1	148
3L-00	1.300	A/C/C	5.1	148	3-00	1.150	A/C/C	5.5	160
1514	1.379	X7	6.8	197	1516	1.403	75	7.3	212
1516	1.403	75	7.3	212	1614	1.153	X7	7.7	223
Group Y7									
1000	1.000	A/C/E	5.7	165					
1100	1.100	A/C/E	5.1	148					
1000	1.000	X10	5.3	154					
1000	1.000	NAV	5.1	149					
3-00	1.150	A/C/C	5.5	160					
1000	1.000	Rdln	5.7	165					
1614	1.153	X7	7.7	223					
1616	1.079	75	8.4	244					

A/C/E Aluminum/Carbon/Extreme
X10 X10 Shafts (Aluminum/Carbon)
Nav Navigator (Aluminum/Carbon)
A/C/C Aluminum/Carbon/Composite
Rdln Redline C2 Carbon-composite
X7 X7 Eclipse and Cobalt (7178 alloy)
75 XX75 Platinum Plus, Blues, Jazz and Neos (7075 alloy)

Note: Shaft Weight at 29" is shown on our Shaft Selection Charts. To determine weight at your shaft length, multiply the grains-per-inch (gpi) by your actual shaft length not including point, insert, or UNI Bushing.

The youth target chart is used the same way as the adult chart except this is set up for recurve (and longbows) only. Find your draw weight in the right hand column and slide left over to your draw length. Again, we recommend that you get your arrows uncut, which requires them to be in one spine group stiffer (upward) for every inch longer than your actual draw length.

them for you. If not, shops will do it for $1-2 per arrow. When my students bend a lot of their arrows I bring my straightening jig to a lesson and teach them to straighten them themselves.

Getting Accessories

Armguard Buy the largest one you can find (<$12). Required for all beginners. Make sure it is relatively easy to put on and adjust. You want it to be snug enough it doesn't move around, but not so tight it cuts off your blood circulation. I personally hate the ones with Velcro fasteners (they get all tangled and stuck together), but you may like them.

Finger Tab I recommend the Wilson Brothers *Black Widow* Tab (<$12, often <$10). Strongly recommended for all beginners. A good tab is worth the cost. Get two if you can afford it. (They are easy to lose!) The tab should be slightly taller than your three string fingers in height. This is because the string wraps around both your top and bottom fingers. If none of the sizes is the exact right fit, buy one that is slightly too large and trim it down with a pair of sharp scissors.

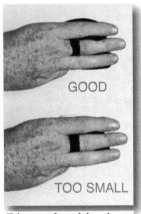

GOOD

TOO SMALL

Tabs must fit and there has to be enough material to cover part of the top of your top finger and bottom of your bottom finger (the string wraps around your fingers.

Chest Protector If you really want one, be sure to try it on before buying it. If it is large enough, but not too large, you may still have to make it fit better with safety pins, paper clips, scissors and needle and thread, whatever works.

Quiver For a first quiver there are Nylon quivers with a single pouch that you can slide onto a belt you already own for around $20. (Nylon web belts can be had in sporting good stores for $2-3.) If your budget is tight, you can put this off and use a ground quiver or just lay your arrows on the ground next to where you are shooting. Some of the world's best archers started out with less.

Bow Case Many people buy a bow case to keep their bow and other gear in. These range from Nylon cloth cases (cheaper) to plastic molded cases (more expensive) to aluminum cases (with wheels!) that cost well over a hundred dollars. There are also archery back packs, and, and. . . .

Tools If you don't have any archery tools yet, keep an eye out for a set of Allen wrenches and a "bow square." (Trust me, you'll need it.)

You don't have to have everything now. One of the nice things about being an archer is there is always something to get you as a birthday (or graduation or other occasion) present.

Often the first purchase is a tab (so it can be personalized). Next most important to get is a bow. Then arrows. Then the other stuff as you need it.

Okay, I've Got My Gear, Now What?

The purpose of getting your own gear is not for pride of ownership or bragging rights. It is so it can be carefully fitted to you. If you got a compound bow, both the draw weight and draw length can be fitted. If you got a recurve bow or longbow, the draw weight and/or brace height (distance from string to bow) can be adjusted. First you have to shoot it a bit and based on your shooting form, your coach will recommend more or less draw weight, more or less brace height, or more or less draw length.

Tuning Using some simple shooting tests, your coach can help you tailor your arrows for maximum accuracy. The big factor is length of the arrow. We got the arrows full length, so we can cut them a bit to make them the exact spine needed to fit you and your bow. (Making arrows shorter makes them stiffer.) Your coach may be able to cut your arrows, but if not, an archery shop can. Other changes can be made as well. Getting everything to work together is called "setting up your bow" (actually bow *and* arrows). The final fine tweaking of your setup is called "tuning."

Having a bow and arrow fit to you and your shooting ability is the real secret to accuracy. Oh, that and practice!

Chapter 5 Q & A s

Q My coach says that "you can't buy better scores" every time I talk about getting something new. What's up with that?

A That's Coaching Wisdom 101 material there. What he/she is trying to convince you of is that consistent accuracy comes from practice and mental focus, not from fancy gear.

This is a bit of "archery wisdom" that isn't even true. If your arrows are all mis-sized and bent, replacing them with a new set will make your scores go up every time. So, you can buy better scores. This "saying," though, does apply when you have good equipment properly fit to you. From that point, the only way to better scores is through practice and mental focus.

Q I have a friend who says there are about a dozen ways to tune my bow. Should I try them?

A Until you can shoot really, really well, tuning is best done with simple bare shaft testing and not much else. There are dozens of tuning techniques because there are thousands of elite archers who are looking for an edge over their competitors. I don't think anybody needs more than two tuning techniques, as long as one of them is "group testing." Group testing is checking whether the size of your groups goes up (worse) or down (better) when you make a change . . . with three or four groups . . . shot at three or four distances . . . for each test. You can see why people want to invent easier ways to tune. But, group testing is still the "Rolls Royce" of tuning tests.

Q Many of the other kids with their own gear have carbon arrows. Do they have an unfair advantage?

A No, just bigger pocketbooks. Strike fear in their little hearts by beating them with aluminum arrows!

Q I have an aunt who wants to give me her old archery stuff. Can it be fit so I can use it?

A Typically adult equipment cannot be adjusted "down" for kids. It is too heavy, has too much draw weight, and cutting arrows shorter makes them less suitable, not more. If you want the equipment to use later, you need to explain to your aunt that you won't be using her gear right away. She will probably understand that you have to "grow into it."

Q My friend got a new bow and he says he shoots a whole bunch better. Will that work for me?

A Sometimes it will. If your "old bow" is the wrong size, wrong weight, or wrong draw weight and the new bow gets all of these things right, it will definitely improve your scores. But realize that the top archers are at the top year after year after year. And each year their bow sponsor gives them a new bow. So, do you think it is it the bow or the archer? (It's the archer. Same archer, different bow, still wins consistently. This has been proven over and over.)

Hey, I like getting new gear, but the only time new gear makes things better is when my old gear was somehow limiting my performance. That doesn't happen too often. (I still like new stuff, I just don't expect it to make me much better.) Practice can make you better a lot cheaper. (And I know you didn't want to hear this.)

(*Yeah, this is the same question as in Chapter 4, but you might have skipped over it there, you know*!)

Archery 4 Kids

Chapter 6
Competing!

One of the wonderful things about target archery is that it is an "open sport." What this means is that you almost never have to qualify for a competition by shooting a high score or winning some other tournament. If you want to compete, all you have to do is send in a registration form and a small fee and show up.

I once shot with a young man at the California State Championships. It was his very first archery tournament! But hey, just because you can do this, doesn't mean it is a good idea. Even so, just attending a tournament and competing can be a good experience, so there is no harm.

This is the USA Archery National Championships and, yes, those are "beginner bows" being used (quite expertly). Don't let anyone tell you those bows aren't any good.

If you want to learn how to win, I always suggest you start with smaller, local tournaments because part of learning how to win is . . . winning. That may sound stupid, but it is essential that you be able to compare the differences between what, for you, is a winning performance and what is not. Maybe a better way to say this is "to learn how to win consistently, you have to win something along the way."

In this chapter, I will show you how competitions work.

The Basics of Competing

Archery competitions are sponsored by archery clubs. Archery clubs are affiliated with archery organizations. One of the archery organizations is USA Archery (the Olympic people). Another is the National Field Archery Association. These are the two biggest. There are quite a few others.

Now, here's the deal. You have to be a member of the parent organization to be able to compete for medals. Think about it. If you didn't have to be a member to compete for medals, pretty soon there wouldn't be enough members of archery organizations that support the clubs that maintain and support the ranges the contests are held on. No clubs, no ranges. No ranges, no competitions.

But, you *can* compete without joining . . . as a "Guest." Actually, I recommend this. But, I must warn you. If you shoot a better score than the kid getting the gold medal in your competitive category, you are going to be signing up the next day. (Guests don't get medals, they just get to compete to see how they would do.) If you really like archery competitions, then you need to join one or more of the organizations. They make it relatively easy to join and tend to charge less for kids to be members. The web sites of the archery organizations are listed in the back of the book. You can get more information straight from them.

Also, the organizations often have lists of their archery clubs. Check the lists to see if there is a club near you and consider joining. Archery clubs often support youth programs, including competitive teams! And even if they don't, members get to use the archery range almost any time they want. "Guests" wanting to shoot may need a member to be there with them and/or pay a fee to shoot.

Also check your local business listings (Yellow Pages or Internet) to see if there is an archery range near you.

Finding Out About Competitions

Most archery competitions aren't advertised at all well. The organizers assume that most of the people coming are connected to an archery club or organization and will get notified in the club's newsletter or some such way. Here are the ways *you* can find out.

Archery Organization's Web Sites Often the sponsoring organizations have a "calendar" or list of competitions that local clubs can post to. Certainly the competitions put on directly by the big-time organization will be listed. Look in the back of this book for the web addresses of the organizations.

Local Archery Club Web Sites If there is a local archery club nearby, check to see if they have a web site on which they post their competitions. If not, try calling them and asking. (My guess is they don't "text.")

Local Archery Shops If you have an archery shop anywhere nearby, check their web site or give them a call. Archery shops often sponsor competitions. If all you have is a "big box" sporting goods store, check to see if they have a big archery section (usually it is bowhunting related). If they have even a small indoor archery range, they probably keep track of competitions.

Ask Your Archery Instructor/Coach/Others Much of the communication between archers is "word of mouth." So, a lot of info can be had from talking to other archers and coaches.

The Kinds of Competitions

There are two basic types of competitions with a great many variations. The two types are: target archery and field archery.

Target Archery Target archery is shot on a flat, usually grassy, field. The targets are at just a few different distances. Archery at the Olympic Games is target archery.

Field Archery Field archery is like golf. The targets are laid out so that you shoot a few arrows (1-4) at one target and then move down a trail to the next target in a string. Golf courses are typically 9 or 18 holes. In target archery, courses are typically 14 or 28 targets. Field ranges are often setup so you must shoot uphill, downhill, and on the side of a hill. Every target is at a different distance. These distances can range (for adults) from 20 feet to 80 yards (less for kids).

On these fields there are many archery games that can be shot. These games specify the kinds of targets, the distances, and the rules of shooting. (Look in the back of the book for some examples.) In field archery, games are broken up into a number of "targets" with the number of arrows per target specified, for example "14 NFAA Field targets, 4 arrows per target." From this you can figure out you will be shooting 56 arrows (14 x 4) in that round. In target archery, the distances and numbers of "ends" and the number of arrows per "end." (The word "end" comes from the old practice of putting targets at both ends of the field, shooting at one target, walking down to get your arrows, and shooting back to the original "end" of the field.) For example, "10 ends of 3 arrows" tells you 30 arrows (10 x 3) will be shot. Some times the "game" just has a name, for example "Columbia Round," or "FITA International Round" and these you will have to look up. Check the appendices for a list of typical target rounds.

A popular form of competition is "novelty competitions." These are often simulated hunting games with the targets being lifelike 3-D animals. These shoots are not formal competitions but do have rules, including rules made up by the hosting club. These novelty shoots are typically put on as fundraisers for local clubs. (It takes a lot of work and money to support an archery range.)

Competitive Categories

Every competition has competitive categories. Kids don't usually compete against adults (except in novelty shoots!). Typically boys and girls (and men and women) compete separately. And kids are put into various age groups, like in other youth sports. These groupings vary from organization to organization, so you have to find out what category you will compete in.

Here is an example of one organization's age categories:

USA Archery Age Groups
Yeoman (<8)
Bowman (8-12)
Cub (12-14)
Cadet (15-16)
Junior (16-18)

You need to know how these ages apply, though. For example, you are a Cub for the whole year in which you turn 15! So, if you turn 15 on January 8th, you started the year as a 14-year old, so you are a Cub until December 31st. Andy ou are allowed to jump "up" in competition. A 14-year old can compete with the cadets, the juniors, even the adults. The current Executive Director of USA Archery won a gold medal in the Pan American Games, competing as an adult even though she was only 13! She later became our youngest Olympic archer by competing, as an adult, at the age of 14.

Be aware that these things change. USA Archery is in the process right now (2010) of changing the Cadet and Junior age categories to be more like the international categories:

Cadet (15-17)

Junior (17-20)

Not only because of age and gender, but you will be

NFAA SHOOTING STYLES

If You Shoot ...	and you are an ...	Adult	Young Adult/ Youth/Cub/PeeWee
		FS	FS
		FSL	FSL
		BHFS	FS
		BHFSL	FSL
		BH	BB
		BB	BB
		Trad–RC	BB
		Trad–LB	BB
		FSL–R/L	FSL–R/L

Key — FS = freestyle   FSL = freestyle limited
BH = bowhunter   BHFSL = bowhunter freestyle limited
BHFS = bowhunter freestyle   BB = barebow
Trad-RC = traditional recurve   Trad-LB = traditional longbow
FSL-R/L = freestyle limited–recurve longbow (basically FITA Freestyle)

Note—In the Junior Division—Young Adult *(15-17 years old)*, Youth *(12-14 years old)*, Cub *(under 12 years old)*—there are only four styles recognized—FS, FSL, BB, and FSL-R/L.

separated into additional categories according to the equipment you use. As an example, the NFAA has the following equipment categories:

Note that the number of categories for kids is fewer than for adults (read the bottom of the chart).

Of course <sigh>, every organization has different rules and categories, so you will have to ask a lot of questions.

Competition Logistics

Competitions can last just a part of a day, like a morning or an evening, or they can last all day (most of it, anyway). Major competitions can be multi-day. Typically, major competitions are: two day (over a weekend) or three day (over a long weekend) or week long (usually in the summer when kids are out of school).

You almost always have to drive to a competition, but major ones usually require longer trips. You may have to arrange for overnight stays (at a friend's place or in a hotel) and there are meals, lodging, etc. to plan and pay for. Of course, this means Mom and/or Dad is involved. If you really take to archery competitions, there is a lot of time and effort and support needed from your parents or guardian.

When you attend a competition, you have to show up early, do a little paperwork, have all of the archery gear you need to compete with (bow, arrows, tab, armguard, tools, etc.), you may have to have packed a lunch and brought water to drink. It is like an all-day affair to a park or the beach. There may or may not be food available for purchase at the event.

There will be no "archery repair facility" available. In some sports, like ice hockey or bowling, there is a repair shop on the premises. This only happens in archery when a competition is in an archery shop, in other words, not often. A consequence of this is that archers help one another. If you have an equipment difficulty, don't be surprised if your competitors offer their help, tools, expertise, even offer to lend you replacement bows, arrows, etc. This is one of the nicer aspects of our sport.

There probably won't be emergency medical services available on field. But, accidents are rare and all tournament organizers have a first aid kit handy.

Questions You Need to Ask

Here's a list of the questions you need to get answers for about a competition.

1. What are the date(s) and time(s) of the competition?
2. What is the location?
3. What rules will be used? (You may have to ask a lot of questions to really understand.)
4. What competitive category will you be in?
5. Do you have to be a "Member" or can you shoot as a "Guest."
6. How many arrows are shot per target/end? How many targets/ends?
7. How much does it cost to register?
8. Will there be food available? (You may need to ask what kinds—candy bars aren't exactly competition fuel.)
9. Do you have to be accompanied by a parent? (In some field shoots, they provide adult supervision; in others parents shoot alongside their children; in still others, they want parents to accompany their children around the course.)
10. . . . and any other questions you have!

A lot of kids might be embarrassed to tell others that

they are at their first competition, but I really recommend *you do tell people that you are at your first (or second, or third) competition.* You will be cut some slack if you don't know a rule or something, and you will find other people will "take you under their wing" to help you through. Archery is a very social sport in which there is much talk and fun between and among archers and officials.

Be aware that, in archery as in all other youth sports, you will occasionally encounter poor behavior from other kids and some parents. I strongly urge you to not "get into it" with these people as there is nothing good to come of it. As few as these people are, we still all hope that they will just go away!

Getting the Competitive Bug

So, if you've tried a few competitions and you think you have found your sport, congratulations! If you really think you want to learn to win at archery, things will change. By far, the most people you encounter at competitions are what are called "recreational archers." They are competing just for fun. And while I don't want you to lose the fun, for some people the fun is to be found in winning! If you are like that, there is one thing you need to do—*find a good coach.*

The two important parts of finding a good coach are the "find" and the "good" parts. Finding a coach has not been made easy. The web sites of the archery organizations aren't much help. There is one site which maintains a list of coaches, but it is by no means complete and it is kind of lame. The site is maintained by NADA, the National Alliance for the Development of Archery (one of the "good guys"). Go to *www.teacharchery.org/Find_Archery_Coaches.html* and follow the directions *very care-*

fully and you will find a sortable list of coaches.

Once you find a coach, figuring out whether he/she is a good one is also hard. It would be nice to have a coach with more training (a USA Archery Level 3 or 4 coach or an NFAA Master Coach) but, at least at the beginning, that may not be necessary. Here are some tips:

Good Coaches Do . . .
1. Good coaches ask a lot of questions.
2. Good coaches explain what they are asking you to do.
3. Good coaches give clear instructions.
4. Good coaches point you toward other resources.
5. Good coaches are well organized.
6. Good coaches focus only on you during your lessons (not your parents or other people).
7. Good coaches know a lot about archery and training and can find out the things they don't know.
8. Good coaches know a lot of other coaches and archers.
      . . . and a lot more.

Good Coaches Don't . . .
1. Good coaches don't yell.
2. Good coaches don't ask "what are you working on?" because they take notes or remember.
3. Good coaches don't miss appointments. (Hey, it does happen. I have even done it myself. My policy is if I miss a lesson, your next lesson is free. No excuses.)
4. Good coaches don't confuse you.
5. Good coaches don't fail to find out the things they don't know.
6. Good coaches don't give commands (except in the case of immediate danger).
7. Good coaches don't ignore your parents or guardian.

8. Good coaches don't ignore your questions.
                        . . . and a lot more.

You should ask about your coach's training. Many "coaches" have no training as a coach, just as an archer. Coaching and shooting are quite different. I suggest you find a coach with some coach training. The basic coach training certificates are Basic Archery Instructor and Intermediate Archery Instructor. The Basic Archery Instructor training (also called a "Level 1" training) was designed to prepare nonarchers to assist in pre-existing archery programs, like summer camps. The Intermedi-ate Archery Instructor training (also called a "Level 2" training) is designed to prepare archers and holders of Basic Instructor/Level 1 certificates to run youth archery programs.

There are fewer than 200 USAA Level 3 and Level 4, and NFAA Master Coaches in the U.S. So, you will have to be lucky to have one of them close.

The fact that the coach has a certificate does not guarantee you have found a good coach and certificates do expire. But having a certificate says your coach is interested enough to spend his/her time and money to learn how to coach. (I have spent several thousand dollars and weeks of my time getting my coach certificates. For example, my Level 3 and Level 4 certificate trainings were held at the Olympic Training Center in Southern California and lasted a week, each.)

Of course, you are going to want to ask all of the logistics questions, too. How much does the coach charge? What times are they available? Where will the lessons be? Does a parent or guardian need to be there? (We teach our coach trainees to never coach alone. We consider having a parent/guardian present very desirable.)

Chapter 6 Q & A

Q A friend of mine said there was math involved in archery. Was he fooling with me?

A Well, there is some arithmetic involved. You have to be able to add up arrow scores to get "end totals" and add those up to get "total scores." That is about it. And, if you make a math error, there are penalties. Most organizations allow kids to use calculators and such, but I guarantee that if you bring one with you out onto a range, you will get teased. Save the calculator for the end of the shoot; there is usually an amount of time allowed after you are done to hand in your score cards.

Q I want to be a State Champion. Any recommendations?

A Just like you don't want to jump into the deep end of the pool to learn how to swim, you are better off starting small, that is at local tournaments. There is a lot more to learn than what I could squeeze into this book but you can learn it as you go. The best thing you can do is to find a good coach.

Q I really like competing (well, winning—I like winning). How do I know if I have the talent to be a really good archer?

A There is only one talent you need. You don't have to be tall, short, fast, slow, big, small, agile, flexible, strong or weak. You need to be able to relax under the tension of the draw and even that can be learned. The only thing you really need is . . . *to like to practice*. That's it. There is no such thing as a talent for archery. It takes hard work and that occurs in practice.

   If you don't like to practice, you can still enjoy archery. You just won't be a consistent winner.

Q At the last shoot I attended I had to shoot "Guest" because I couldn't prove I was a member. That doesn't seem fair. Why wouldn't they just take my word for it?

A Welcome to the real world. If you weren't aware, people do lie. (Other people lie, that is, I am sure you are honest!) Most of the rules of competition, in my humble opinion, exist because somebody tried to cheat. And "fair" is applying the rules to everyone the same way.

Also, this is why the associations/organizations issue membership cards.

Q My local archery shop doesn't want to answer my questions. Why are they so grouchy?

A Most archery shops are quite helpful, especially with beginners. But do realize their job is to sell archery stuff and if you aren't buying any or haven't bought much, they are going to spend their time with their "real" customers. This shows you the advantage of having a coach. The coach is being paid to answer your questions, the shop employee is not (so cut them a little slack).

Q My coach spends most of his time talking to his girl-friend and the shop people. What should I do?

A Find another coach, a good one.

Q My coach keeps answering my questions with other questions. Why can't I get some answers?

A If you can answer his/her questions, you will have answered your own. He/she is teaching you to think through archery situations on your own.

But, I agree, a steady diet of this can get a little irritating. Ask your coach if you can take turns. One lesson he answers your questions with questions and the next

110

he/she answers with answers. It is always good to take turns. (I am trying to teach you that the relationship between coach and athlete is always being discussed . . . at least between good coaches . . . and good athletes.)

Steve Ruis

Appendices

For Learning More

Freebies

There are a great many free archery resources available online. Here are but a few:

- *Easton Archery Spine Chart* (available online from Easton Archery Products, *www.eastonarchery.com*, look under "Company" then "Downloads")
- *Easton Arrow Tuning Manual* (this was once available online free from Easton Archery Products and may still be (*www.eastonarchery.com*, look under "Company" then "Downloads" or do a web search for "Easton Arrow Tuning Guide" and it is available in multiple places) and was available in print form for a nominal charge.
- *FITA Rule Book* The FITA Rule Book (used by USA Archery) and much more is available at *www.archery.org*. Look under "Rules" and "Publications."
- Reference *Guide for Recurve Archers* by Murray Elliot (available online for free, Google it) This is full of good, solid technical knowledge for recurve bow archers and coaches.

Books

- *Simple Maintenance for Archery* by Ruth Rowe and Alan Anderson Everyone who wants to be able to adjust and maintain their own archery gear needs a copy of this book! Step-by-step procedures for building arrows, tying on nocking point locators, replacing center servings, etc. (available from *www.qproductsarchery.com*)

- *Archery Fundamentals* by Doug Engh A good basic introduction to archery (available at most bookstores). This is a perfect resource for parents of beginning archers. Doug is the president of NADA.
- *Fundamentals of Recurve Target Archery* by Ruth Rowe Great resource for recurve target archers and parents on how to start on a good path (available from *www.qproductsarchery.com*)
- *Field Archery, A Complete Guide* by Michael Hamlett-Wood The writer is British so the focus is on their practices and rules, which aren't so different from anyone else's.
- *Traditional Archery* by Sam Fadala A good start if you, like me, started out knowing very little about traditional archery, U.S. style (available from Stackpole Books, 800.READ-NOW).

If you don't want to have to buy these, check your local library. If they don't have a title you want, ask them to acquire it.

A Kid's Guide to Archery Terms

There are a great many archery terms. Here is a shorter list useful to beginners.

Archery Terms with Definitions

Anchor point   The reference point that a person pulls the bow string to before releasing. This point should be the same for each shot and may be the side of the mouth, corner of the chin, or other reference point.

Armguard   Device attached to the forearm of the arm to protect it from a string burn or keeps the sleeve from catching on the string.

Arrow shaft   The main body of the arrow before the nock, fletching, or point is installed. It can be made from several materials including wood, aluminum, carbon, and composites.

Arrow shelf   The area of the bow above the handle or grip where the arrow sits.

Arrow straighter   A tool used to straighten arrow shafts which are only slightly bent.

Back of the Bow   The side farthest away from you when you hold bow in shooting position.

Bare shaft   A arrow shaft without fletching.

Belly/Face	The side closest to you when you hold the bow in shooting position.
Bow square	Tool that is T-shaped used to determine where to place string nock locators, measure brace height, and tiller.
Bow string	Several strands of material twisted together to form a strong string used to launch an arrow.
Bow stringer	An aid that helps to prevent limb twist and tip damage while installing the bow string.
Boyer	A person who makes bows.
Brace height	The distance from the string to the deepest part of the handle or grip. This distance can be changed by twisting the string tighter to increase the height and untwisting it to decrease the height. Also called "string height."
Cable guard	The rod on compound bows which keeps the cables away from the center of the bow so the arrow can pass by without hitting the cables.
Cam	The wheel or pulley on the end of compound bow's limb used to provide let-off and power. They may be round, elliptical, or very complex in shape.
Clicker	A device attached to the bow which clicks when you are at your desired anchor point.
Cock feather/ vane	The odd colored or marked feather/vane which faces away from the bow when the arrow is on the string. Also called the "index feather/vane." Compound bow

arrow rests may require a different orientation.

Compound bow A bow with one or two cams which provide let-off and power.

Crossbow Bolt The shaft or arrow fired from a crossbow.

Crossbow A small, strong bow, held and shot like a rifle. The stronger one's have a device to help cock it.

Dacron A type material used to make bowstrings.

D-Loop A string in a U shape tied on the bow string around the nock point that a release aid is attached to when shooting.

Draw length The distance a person draws a bow, measured from the bottom of the arrow nock to 1¾″ past the arrow rest (approximately the back of a bow) when in shooting position.

Draw weight Amount of pull force measured in pounds that it takes to pull a bow string a certain distance.

Fast Flight A lightweight material that has little stretch and is used to make bowstrings for newer bows.

Field points Points that are round with a sharp point, usually used for field archery and hunting practice.

Finger pinch Having your fingers pinched against each other and the arrow's nock by the bow string when pulling the string back (typically due to a bow which is too short).

Fistmele An older term for the brace/string height.

Fletching clamp The clamp that the fletching is placed into before being attached to a fletching jig.

Fletching jig	A tool used to hold the fletching clamp(s) which apply fletching to an arrow shaft.
Fletching	The feathers or vanes used to stabilize an arrow in flight.
Ground quiver	A piece of archery equipment that holds arrows. It may be stuck into the ground or merely rest upon it.
Index feather/vane	See Cock feather/vane.
Insert	An arrow part that accepts the screw in point or a nock.
Kisser button	A button placed on a bow string to hold your anchor point consistently in the same position.
Let-off	The percent that a bow's holding weight is reduced from its pulling weight when a compound bow is properly drawn fully.
Limb tip notch	The notches at the end of the bow limbs where the bow string is placed. Also called a "string groove."
Limb	The parts of the bow that bend when the string is pulled back.
Longbow	An archery bow with no cams and when strung, the string only touches at the limb tip notches.
Nock	Arrow part glued onto or pressed into the back of an arrow shaft that the bow string fits into. On early or very traditional arrows, the nock is cut into the shaft itself.
Nocking pliers	Special pliers used to install or remove brass bowstring nocking point locators.

Nocking
point locator   A mark put on bow string to mark the nocking point of the arrow. Sometimes a simple knot in a string is used, sometimes the point is marked with a brass clip with a plastic insert.

Nocking point   The spot on bow string where the arrow nock is placed to be shot.

Peep sight   The rear sight of a compound bow. A piece of metal, plastic, or rubber with a hole in it placed into the string, which then allows the archer to look through the string.

Quiver   A piece of archery equipment that holds arrows. It may be attached to the bow, placed on a belt, or carried on your shoulder or back.

Recurve bow   A bow that has no cams which when strung is such that the string contacts the bow limbs a short distance from the limb tips.

Release   Letting go of the string to shoot an arrow.

Release aid   A tool that is used to pull the bow string and provide a better release by a trigger of some type.

Riser/handle   The middle part of a bow that has the grip, shelf, sight window and other parts. Also called the "handle."

Serving jig   A tool used to apply serving string to bowstrings and cables.

Serving   String material applied to the bow string to in the nock area to make the string last longer (center serving) and used also to

119

make a loop in the string ends (end serving).

Shooting glove
A three-fingered leather glove used to protect the fingers while shooting bows. Not recommended for target archers.

Sight window
The area of the bow above the grip and arrow shelf where you would mount a bow sight.

Spin tester
A tool that checks the straightness of an arrow by spinning it.

Spine
A term that describes the stiffness of an arrow shaft and tells if the shaft is strong enough to be shot in a bow of known poundage. Too light or too stiff arrows can cause erratic arrow flight.

Stabilizer
A rod of various lengths and weights that is attached to a bow to make for a more stable bow and, secondarily, to reduce vibrations from shot arrows.

Tab
A small piece of material placed between fingers and string to protect the fingers while shooting a bow and to provide a slick surface for the string to slide from.

Take down bow
A long bow or recurve bow which can be taken apart for transportation usually into two or three pieces.

Tiller
The distance from the string perpendicular to each limb at the ends of the riser/handle. These measurements can be adjusted on modern recurve and compound bows.

Tuning
Making small adjustments to bow and/or arrows to make a bow perform at its optimal level.

Types of Archery Targets / Scoring

There are a great many different ways to shoot arrows from a bow. First, there are different kinds of bows, then there are quite a different number of techniques to be used in shooting any one of the kinds. For example, for just compound bow archers, the National Field Archery Association recognizes six shooting styles (*see table on page 103 for more detail*):

Freestyle
Freestyle Limited
Bowhunter
Bowhunter Freestyle
Bowhunter Freestyle Limited, and
Barebow

and this is just one association (and there are others for recurve and longbow archers)! Then there are the divisions (Youth (3-4 age groups), Adult, Seniors (2 age groups)) and gender (male-female). Each of these shooting styles has its own set of rules in addition to the common rules all archers must follow in competition.

Then there are differences in targets shot at. Most associations have created their own targets. In most cases, the distinction is not *where* to shoot (if the target is paper, try the middle) but in how to score it. USA Archery has targets with 10 scoring rings (worth 1-10 points, sensibly) while the NFAA has targets with five scoring rings (worth 1-5 points) but somehow left off the rings worth one and two points on many of their targets making them 5-4-3-0 targets (*see the diagrams*).

Many archers shoots simulated hunting scenarios with three dimensional (3-D) targets (life-like turkeys and deer, etc.). There are several different scoring schemes associated with these animal targets.

As a general rule, if an arrow touches a higher scoring ring on a target, it gets the higher score. For more details on scoring consult the organizations themselves.

It is important to note that human or humanoid targets are never used in archery. Young students have a great deal of fun making up their own targets to shoot at, but they may not represent human beings.

Unfortunately, each archery organization tends to develop its own kinds of targets. Here are examples of the common ones used throughout competitive archery in the U.S. and around the world.

USA Archery / FITA

USA Archery, the national governing body for Olympic-style archery in the U.S. uses the targets designated by FITA. They come in various sizes but this one is typical (*left*).

FITA also sponsors field archery tournaments and uses a target similar to the NFAA "Hunter" target (*right*).

FITA
"Target"
Target

FITA
"Field"
Target

NFAA

The National Field Archery Association uses targets unique to that organization and which have been adopted around the world by the International Field Archery Association (IFAA). The primary targets come in two styles: "Field" targets and "Hunter" targets. The Field targets are shot at multiples of five(5) yards distance. The Hunter targets are shot at multiples of one (1) yard distance. The NFAA also has "paper" animal targets (to distinguish them from 3-D animal targets), which are scored differently.

NFAA
"Field"
Target

NFAA
"Hunter"
Target

NFAA
"Animal" Target

ASA / IBO / NFAA
3-D Animal Targets

There are various scoring schemes for shooting animal targets, check with the organizations for theirs.

Archery Organizations

There are a great many archery organizations, most of which go by their initials. Here is a guide to them. Most have websites from which you may be able to get useful information. (Website addresses and phone numbers subject to change.)

ASA (Archery Shooters Association, *www.asaarchery.com*, 770.795.0232) An organization of professional and amateur archers which sponsors (unmarked distance) 3-D tournaments in the U.S. (simulated hunting scenarios).

FITA (Federation Internationale a Tir a l'Arc/ International Archery Federation) Governs Olympic style archery internationally. Sponsors target archery competitions under Olympics and as world and continental championships. You can download their rule book (for free) from their website *http://archery.org* (look under "Rules").

IBO (International Bowhunters Organization, *www.ibo.net*, 440.967.2137) An organization of professional and amateur archers which sponsors mostly (unmarked) 3-D competitions in the eastern U.S.

IFAA (International Field Archery Association) Governs field archery internationally. Overlaps with FITA as FITA has a field division. Sponsors target and field archery competitions indoors and out as world and continental championships.

JOAD (Junior Olympic Archery Development Program, *http://usarchery.org/programs/joad-youth-archery*, 727.389.3264) USA Archery's youth program. The only archery-only youth program that is reasonably completely developed. This is where the action is in youth competitive teams. Takes teams of Junior and Cadet archers overseas for competition. Has youth only national championships (almost all other organizations allow youths to compete at the same time as adults, but JOAD has "kids only" competitions, the way it should be). Contact USA Archery directly.

NAA   (National Archery Association *aka* USA Archery—see below) Governs Olympic-style archery in U.S. NGB (national governing body) for FITA; also has compound archers who compete up to the FITA world championships, but not in the Olympics. Sponsors target and field archery competitions indoors and out. See USAA.

NADA   (National Alliance for the Development of Archery, *www.teacharchery.com*, 352.472.2388) Created to foster the growth of archery in the U.S. Is rapidly becoming the U.S. archery coach's association. Coordinates the training of Level 1 and 2 coaches for the NAA and NFAA as well as for NASP, the Air Force, and other entities.

NASP   (National Archery in the Schools Program) A U.S. organization begun in Kentucky and promulgated through state fish and game departments to sponsor short-term archery in PE classes in grammar and high schools. Now in all 50 states and still growing.

NFAA   (National Field Archery Association, *www.nfaa-archery.org*, 605.260.9279) Governs field archery in U.S. NGB (national governing body) for IFAA. Sponsors target, 3-D, and field archery competitions indoors and out.

USAA   (USA Archery, *www.usarchery.org*, 719.866.4576) Formerly just the name of that part of the NAA that was the National Governing Body (NGB) or official representative of the U.S. to FITA. Recently the NAA has adopted this as the name of the entire organization. USA Archery uses the rules of FITA in its competitions.

Some Individual Competition Rounds
Outdoor Rounds
(*see table at right*)

Archery 4 Kids

	Men	Women	Youths
NFAA Hunter Round	14 targets, four arrows per target, scored 5-4-3 on NFAA Hunter targets in 1 yd increments	same	Shot from shorter distances based on age
NFAA Field Round	14 targets, four arrows per target, scored 5-4-3 on NFAA Field targets in 5 yd increments	same	Shot from shorter distances based on age
NFAA Animal Round	14 targets, 1-3 arrows per target, scored based on first scoring arrow on NFAA Animal (paper) targets in 1 yd increments	same	Shot from shorter distances based on age
FITA International Round	6x6 arrows at 90 and 70 meters at 122 cm target, then 12x3 arrows at 50 and 30 meters at 80 cm target, scored 10-0	same as for men except the distances are 70, 60, 50, and 30 meters	Shot from shorter distances based on age
American Round (900 Round)	5x6 arrows at 60, 50, and 40 yards, scored 10-0 on 122 cm FITA target	same	Shot from shorter distances based on age
Metric 900 Round (FITA 900)	5x6 arrows at 60, 50, and 40 meters, scored 10-0 on 122 cm FITA target	same	Shot from shorter distances based on age

Indoor Rounds

	Men	Women	Youths
NFAA 300 Round	12x5 arrows at 20 yards, at the 40 cm target scored 5,4,3 (or NFAA five spot)	same	same
Vegas 300 Round	10x3 arrows at 18 meters, scored 10-0 on 40 cm FITA target (or triangular three spot)	same	same
FITA 18 m	10x3 arrows scored 10-0 on 40 cm FITA target	same	same
FITA 25 m	10x3 arrows scored 10-0 on 60 cm FITA target	same	same

Historic Outdoor Rounds

	Men	Women	Youths
York Round	12x6 arrows at 100 yards, 8x6 arrows at 80 yards, 4x6 arrows at 60 yards, at the 122 cm target scored 9,7,5,3,1,0	N/A	N/A
Hereford Round	N/A	12x6 arrows at 80 yards, 8x6 arrows at 60 yards, 4x6 arrows at 50 yards, at the 122 cm target scored 9,7,5,3,1,0	N/A
American Round	5x6 arrows at 60, 50, and 40 yards, scored 9,7,5,3,1,0 on 122 cm FITA target	same	N/A
Columbia Round	N/A	4x6 arrows at 50, 40, 30 yards, scored 9,7,5,3, 1,0 on 122 cm FITA target	N/A
Metropolitan Round	5x6 arrows at 100, 80, 60, 50, 40 yards, scored 9,7,5,3,1,0 on 122 cm FITA target	5x6 arrows at 60, 50, 40, 30 yards, scored 9,7,5,3, 1,0 on 122 cm FITA target	5x6 arrows at 40, 30, 20 yards, scored 9,7,5,3, 1,0 on 122 cm FITA target
National Round	N/A	8x6 arrows at 60 yards, 4x6 arrows at 50 yards, scored 9,7,5,3,1,0 on 122 cm FITA target	N/A

Steve Ruis

Made in the USA
Lexington, KY
18 December 2019